SARAH JESSICA PARKER

SARAH JESSICA PARKER

Marc Shapiro

ECW PRESS

The publication of *Sarah Jessica Parker* has been generously supported
by The Canada Council, the Ontario Arts Council, and the Government
of Canada through the Book Publishing Industry Development Program.

CANADIAN CATALOGUING IN PUBLICATION DATA

Shapiro, Marc, 1949-
Sarah Jessica Parker
Includes bibliographical references.
ISBN 1-55022-467-0
1. Parker, Sarah Jessica
2. Motion picture actors and actresses—United States—Biography.
3. Television actors and actresses—United States—Biography. I. Title.
PN2287.P27S52 2001   791.43′028′092   C2001-900537-7

Cover and interior design by Guylaine Régimbald — SOLO DESIGN.
Typesetting by Yolande Martel.
This book is set in Electra and Basilea.

Printed by Transcontinental.

Distributed in Canada by General Distribution Services,
325 Humber College Boulevard, Etobicoke, Ontario M9W 7C3.

Distributed in the United States by LPC Group,
1436 West Randolph Street, Chicago, IL 60607, U.S.A.

Distributed in Europe by Turnaround Publisher Services, Unit 3,
Olympia Trading Estate, Coburg Road, Wood Green, London, N2Z 6T2.

Distributed in Australia and New Zealand by Wakefield Press,
17 Rundle Street (Box 2266), Kent Town, Adelaide, South Australia 5071.

Published by ECW PRESS
Suite 200
2120 Queen Street East
Toronto, Ontario M4E 1E2
Canada.

ecwpress.com

PRINTED AND BOUND IN CANADA

THIS BOOK IS DEDICATED TO

My wife Nancy: We'll always have Paris. My daughter Rachael: You deserve the life you're living. Agent Lori Perkins: The straw that stirs the drink. Robert Lecker: For the chance. Bennie, Freda, Selma: The family. Mike Kirby and Steve Ross: The voices from the underground. Keri, Chaos, and Bad Baby: The pets in the hood. And finally to Sarah Jessica Parker: For the good life.

TABLE OF CONTENTS

# Introduction

Cinderella Lives

I'm not big on fables. Prefab happy endings have always made me uncomfortable. But I've always liked Cinderella. As a fairy tale, it contains all the classic elements. The downtrodden good girl who overcomes huge odds to triumph over seemingly insurmountable adversity. The magic. The ideal of finding true love and, of course, that age-old notion of living happily ever after.

It is no wonder that Hollywood, the studios as well as the celebrity media, has been quick to ascribe the phrase "Cinderella Story" to any actress who has come out of nowhere to capture our collective fancy. In nearly all cases, the hype has usually fallen prey to the reality and has diminished the power of the "Cinderella" tag. Let's face it, most of these so-called Cinderellas did not have it that hard. You don't qualify as a Cinderella if you've chipped a nail. If your trust fund subsidized a couple of years in Off Off Broadway until you lucked into a Cruise picture because of your dad's connections, you're not a Cinderella. If you . . . well I think you get the picture. Measuring up to Cinderella is not easy.

And then there's Sarah Jessica Parker . . . who could not be more like Cinderella if she tried. Much like the popular vision of that fairy-tale princess, Sarah is an unconventional beauty right out of a Raphael painting. Large expressive eyes, cascading ringlets of long blonde hair, and a slight and athletic body combine to exude a subtle sexuality that seems to be perpetually surrounded by mists. She did not have a wicked stepmother and evil stepsisters. But growing up in a fragmented and poor family for which money was often nonexistent and things like electricity were always being shut off was, for Sarah, the real-world equivalent of being down on her knees scrubbing floors. Sarah did not dream of dressing up and going to the ball in a fairy-dust-induced coach and four horses. Her dreams were steeped in the arts, dance, music, and acting and were encouraged by her real fairy godmother—her mother, Barbara.

Like Cinderella, Sarah eventually got to go to the ball and met her prince. But when the clock struck midnight, she did not return to rags. Instead, she went on to live a fairy-tale existence, with equal amounts of triumph, disappointment, and adventure. Sarah remained very much a girl-woman in both her physical beauty and her attitude. Reluctant to date a lot and far from being a party girl, she seemed to the world at large enticingly chaste and shy in an old-fashioned sort of way. Along the way, Sarah did find love, albeit fleeting and often troubled, with a variety of suitors that included Robert Downey Jr., Nicolas Cage, and John F. Kennedy Jr. But it would be years before her true Prince Charming, Matthew Broderick, would come into her life and fulfill her dreams of love.

Oh yeah. That happy ending I was talking about? It came from a rather unlikely place in 1998 when Sarah was offered the starring role in an edgy, real-world fable called *Sex and the City*. But this fairy tale does not end here. For while Sarah has gathered up all the perks that go with Hollywood stardom, she has remained very much the wide-eyed innocent who went to the ball more than 25 years ago. She has given up smoking in favor of her favorite candy, M&Ms. She no longer swears. One last holdout, the F-word, was given up as part of a New Year's resolution in 2000. Now the worst you get is the occasional "jeez." The word "grace" appears on her computer screensaver as a constant reminder to be nice to people.

Her no-nudity edict is still intact. And, despite having more money than she knows what to do with, Sarah will still occasionally balk at the idea of making a pricey purchase; the memory of her struggling years is permanently stamped in her psyche. On the set of *Sex and the City*, she is unimaginably down to earth and unaffected. Despite sharing a producer credit on the show, Sarah is very much the den mother of the cast and crew. She often lobbies for a day off when she thinks the crew is overworked. She shows up on time, knows her lines, and never presents herself as anything more than part of the gang.

These traits have extended to her relationship with Broderick, which evolved from a live-in relationship beginning in 1992 to the eventual fairy-tale marriage in 1997. As a couple, they live surprisingly normal lives devoted to simple pleasures like bike riding, shopping, baseball games, and the theater. Unlike so many Hollywood relationships, theirs seems to have "happily ever after" written all over it.

In a world that thrives on rumor and innuendo, Sarah is scandal-free. By her own estimation, she is boring. But "boring" is the wrong word. "Classy" is a much better one. She is someone who quietly goes about her business and her life in a fashion that is at once too good to be true and yet utterly believable in a down-home Middle America sort of way. Sarah would not know how to put on airs if she tried. "Cynical" is not in her vocabulary. Personally and professionally, people have taken notice of her sly, enthusiastic sensuality, her serious demeanor that often dissolves into childlike laughter, and her overall sense of peace and serenity. Many have found her the delightful next link in an acting lineage to Goldie Hawn. That is high praise indeed. But to the people who have gotten to know her, she is simply Sarah.

To dismiss the life of Sarah Jessica Parker as just another rags-to-riches story is to overlook the obvious—that attention to one's craft is ultimately its own reward. Yes, it is a fairy tale. But while the parallels between Cinderella and Sarah are many, there remains that all-important difference. Cinderella is a story with an ending. For Sarah, putting on the glass slipper was only the beginning.

—Marc Shapiro, 2001

Hard Times   1

The world was in a funny place in the early 1960s. People who had known wars, depressions, and the horrors of dictators on foreign shores had long since settled in for a long winter's nap of prosperity and not-too-veiled materialism. But there were storm clouds on the horizon. People who were tired of sitting in the back of the bus were infuriated. There were the first rumblings of "equal pay for equal work" and "make love not war." Even what passed for rock and roll was way too vanilla.

If you blinked on the road to the revolution, you might have easily missed Nelsonville, Ohio. Located in the southeastern corner of Ohio, Nelsonville was the coal-mining center of the state. Strictly blue collar and conservative in its values, it was the kind of town that proudly rolled up its sidewalks at sundown and was big on patriotism and rock-solid religious virtues. It was a town of lunch boxes, 40-hour weeks, and crew cuts. In the most comfortable sense, it was a place where everybody knew everybody else by name. The town of Nelsonville bled red, white, and blue. It seemed like an odd choice for anybody of even moderately liberal views. But Nelsonville was the place that Stephen and Barbara Parker called home.

The Parkers were an idealistic young couple—traditional in their basic values and liberal in their outlook and attitude. They shared a love for the written word, museums, and all things artistic.

They would regularly attend local theater productions and were knowledgeable on the subject of film. They did not run away from questions and answers.

Stephen was an aspiring writer with an entrepreneurial bent who had hopes of making the big time as a journalist. Barbara was a teacher, an arts-inclined free spirit who was big on left-wing politics and the plight of the underdog. The couple had met in college and discovered a mutual love for the artistic side of life and a softness in their souls. They had fallen in love almost immediately and had been married not long after graduation from college. Essentially middle American in temperament, neither had an interest in heading for New York, Chicago, or Los Angeles, which seemed to be ideal places for Stephen to latch onto newspaper or magazine work. They wanted a less stressful environment, and for some unknown reason they settled on Nelsonville.

Stephen and Barbara both believed in large families, and, by the early 1960s, the Parker family was expanding on a yearly basis with the births of Pippen, Timothy, and Rachel. While on the surface the Parkers seemed to be the ideal Midwestern family, an underlying tension was, in fact, already eating away at their relationship and eroding their hopes and dreams. Money always seemed to be at the core of the escalating problems in the Parker household. Stephen's failure to make a go of writing and the time Barbara had to take away from work with the birth of each child put the family constantly on the edge of poverty and homelessness. But it was to the Parkers' credit that their children never went hungry and always had a roof over their heads.

But while they put up a proud front and continued to present themselves as a thriving, prosperous family, the reality was that neither was comfortable with the idea of being poor and having to struggle just to get by. Barbara, in looking back on those times, would readily acknowledge that she felt self-conscious about being poor and having to live a secondhand life and that she suffered a lot of sleepless nights. For Stephen, who would often resort to part-time jobs in order to make ends meet, there were the inevitable frustrations of pursuing a dream but always seeming to come up short—and the guilt that went along with the feeling that he was letting his family down.

Given the family's financial and emotional state, the last thing the Parkers needed was another child. And so it came as a shock when, in 1964, Barbara once again found herself pregnant. The next nine months were a literal roller coaster of emotions for Stephen and Barbara. Some days were better than others, but in the end they shrugged their shoulders at the prospect of a fourth child, figuring they had managed to get by to that point and would, somehow, continue to do so.

A second daughter, Sarah Jessica Parker, was born on March 25, 1965. On the surface, Sarah's birth was welcomed by Stephen and Barbara, and nobody would ever accuse the Parkers of being less than loving, doting parents. But the reality was that Sarah's birth succeeded only in adding another strain to the already tense Parker marriage.

As the bills piled up and the prospects for a better life began to diminish, Stephen began to feel totally trapped amid the ever-expanding family, the chronic poverty, and his own professional failures. Arguments between Stephen and Barbara, as well as long periods in which the couple barely spoke to each other, were common occurrences. With seemingly no light at the end of the tunnel, Stephen chose to walk away from his wife and young children.

Barbara was saddened, disappointed, and bitter at the course that her life with Stephen had taken. But her major concern at that moment was for the children. Barbara took great pains to make sure that her children knew that the breakup was amicable and that her growing brood knew that it was not in any way their fault. The reality was that she had been just as unhappy as Stephen. The love had gone out of their marriage. She could see no good reason for them to stay together, not even for the sake of the children. Within a year, the couple were divorced, and Sarah did not see her father again for many years.

Times continued to be tough. Barbara was virtually house-bound with four young children to care for. She could not work and was unable to support herself and her family. Stephen kicked in a little money now and then, but that soon stopped. There was a real fear that the family would shortly wind up homeless. Barbara could see no other option but to go on welfare. For Barbara, this was a humbling step. She had always been a woman of deep, unbending pride. The stigma from the divorce was bad enough. Adding welfare to the equation would brand them as outcasts in the town they had lived in for years. But, in the short term, Barbara saw it as the only way out.

For Barbara, the process of signing the papers and going through the interviews necessary for the family to get on welfare was painful. For the first time, she saw that look from people—the look that said you're no longer as good as the rest of the hard-working folks of Nelsonville, Ohio.

Barbara's three older children, all under the age of five, had a sense that something had changed in their lives. Their father was not around much, and their mother always seemed to look sad. As a mere toddler, Sarah was effectively insulated from the family's level of misery, as she had been from the divorce. At this age, her world was still four walls, a bottle, and reassuring words from her mother, brothers, and sister. But, with her natural curiosity in place from birth, Sarah would often recall sensing that, during those early years, there was something different about her family. Sarah's personality was formed at a fairly early age, largely due to the influence of her mother and the living conditions that she has, in later years, described as "psychotic." When Sarah was still an infant, she would often be regaled by her mother with tales of César Chávez and his migrant workers' union as well as the plight of oppressed mine workers, thus planting in her the seeds of interest in politics and social justice.

In a house with four children constantly vying for attention, Sarah developed an uncanny ability to amuse herself. She would play with imaginary friends and make up childishly complex games that only she could understand. As the youngest, Sarah was also the willing guinea pig for the antics of her brothers and sister, who, often at the urging of Barbara, would involve her in their games. Inevitably, Sarah would also become involved in high-risk adventures that would drive her mother to distraction. When she was two years old, Sarah had to be rescued by her mother after becoming disoriented while inside a snow tunnel that had been built by her older brothers and sister.

The first word Sarah ever spoke was a big one—"dangerous." It came tumbling out of her mouth one day when she was in the kitchen with her mother and picked up a knife. "When my mother took it from me, I said 'dangerous.'" Sarah also recalled that around age two she attempted to shave with a straight razor. She remembered being "fascinated by it," thinking that the idea of shaving "was cool." So one day "I tried it, and I slit my face open. I was always in trouble."

Since toys were a luxury that Barbara could rarely afford, the children were usually left to their own devices and imaginations to amuse themselves. Sarah's older brother Pippen recalled in a *Los Angeles Times* interview that they would always get together and put on plays for their parents based on books they were reading at the time. Pippen also remembered that his sister was quite the singer. "Since she was two, she was making up songs, and we'd hear her off in her room, singing, about taking a bath, what was for dinner, anything."

The family's fortunes changed when Sarah was three years old and Barbara met a theater arts major named Paul Forste. Forste, eight years Barbara's junior, was much like Stephen: a down-to-earth blue-collar guy, long on creative vision, but also an honest, hard worker with a firm grasp on reality. Paul was exactly the type of man Barbara was looking for. Shortly after, they married, and Forste moved Barbara and her family from Nelsonville to the big, rambling, and somewhat run-down house he owned in a middle-class Cincinnati neighborhood. The move was exciting for the children, but Barbara was a little reluctant. Nelsonville, for better or for worse, was the place where her children had been born and where, in better times, she had made a life with Stephen. But

Paul had already shown himself to be a kind man who had taken her children on as his own. And in Cincinnati, there was the promise of a good life and no more welfare.

Within the year, Barbara found herself pregnant with what would be the first of four children she would have with Paul. Her initial reaction was concern about what yet another mouth to feed would do to this second chance at a life for her family. To her relief, Paul was thrilled with the news. Barbara was confident that she had found a man who was capable of supporting her and her large brood and would not walk out when times got tough. Unfortunately, Forste's luck soon changed. Theater crew work and stage transportation had been a growing business for Paul despite the fact that, in Cincinnati, it was sporadic at best. But eventually there was a downturn in the business, and Paul was forced to take a job as a truck driver in order to make a living. Yet he was still out of work for long periods of time. The family was once again forced to turn to welfare in order to make ends meet. By this time, Barbara was about to give birth to her sixth child, but tensions that had begun with Stephen now continued with a run of economic bad luck for Paul. However, she had learned a lesson from her first marriage: do not duck and run at the first sign of trouble.

By this time, Sarah was old enough to realize that her family did not have all the nice things her friends did, that they had few toys, and that the furniture was not new. She discovered what poverty was without having to have it explained to her. Sarah often described her early childhood in Cincinnati as a page out of Dickens, and the reality often seemed harsh. "I remember being poor," she told the *New York Times*. "There was no great way to hide it. We didn't have electricity sometimes. We didn't have Christmas sometimes and we didn't have birthdays sometimes." And while it was not a pleasant situation, it was one that the Parker children were all too familiar with. Being frugal and cautious had been a way of life for so long that they logically figured that it was the way it would always be and so got used to the idea of always having less and always doing without.

For Sarah, who was still at a formative age, there were moments when she did not understand why they could not have the nice things her friends had. These moments were particularly heart-breaking times for Barbara, who thought she had no choice but to tell her young daughter the truth. There would be no sugar coating in Sarah's world. Another element of her maturing personality was filed away for future reference.

Even when there was a little money in the house, the family still had to think long and hard about any purchases. Barbara remembered hunting for bargains and secondhand items at rummage sales and nearby outlet stores. Sarah and her sisters were each allotted two pairs of shoes for a year, and it was the rare dress that cost more than 99 cents.

Sarah and her siblings had front-row seats on how hard times can be. There were a couple of Christmases when presents consisted of wrapped-up toothbrushes and tubes of toothpaste. She painfully recalled that bill collectors would often knock on the door. She would often pick up the telephone only to hear a voice on the other end threatening to shut their phone service off. Often the children would receive these calls. Watching her parents in long, often heated discussions about which bill to pay and where the money would have to come from formed a lasting impression on Sarah. She learned early on that money is important and that without it she was in for a lot of heartache.

Like just about every element of her life, Sarah's religious upbringing was a bit unorthodox. Sarah always respected her father's religion and considered herself half Jewish, but while the family observed primarily Catholic holidays—Paul was nominally Roman Catholic—their religious attitudes were more internal than specific. Sarah most certainly believed in God, but her pathway to religious enlightenment always seemed to be more progressive than traditional, and it was almost sure to have been influenced by family struggles and lack of money. When the family did go to church, there were those awkward moments when they passed on the collection plate.

Sarah was growing up fast, and those memories would stay

with her forever. The concept of welfare was totally foreign to Sarah until she entered the third grade at The Clifton School in Cincinnati. Because her family was on state relief, she was called up to the front of the lunch line to receive a ticket for a free lunch. It was at this moment that Sarah felt the first sting of embarrassment and shame. "I knew I was different from the kids who pay for lunch or bring their lunch from home," she recalled of that painful time. "It was a stigma thing. I was not the only person receiving a free lunch, but you are aware." The experience would permanently scar Sarah. She had friends in the neighborhood who would come over and play in her yard. But, because she sensed that the old furniture and the mismatched linen inside her house were not as good as what her friends had, she felt ashamed. "I don't ever recall letting our friends into the house."

The constant economic struggles continued to have a psychological impact on Sarah and her siblings. There were times when Barbara and Paul ran out of excuses and would simply tell their children that there was not going to be a Christmas or a birthday present that year. "As kids, we were disappointed," Sarah recalled in *Celebrity Interviews*. "But I was never denied love, food, or shelter. So, occasionally, we wanted a present and there wasn't a present. But my parents gave us so much love that I simply can't be bitter about it."

In later years, Sarah would laughingly describe her upbringing as "progressive." But the reality, which she disclosed in an interview with the *St. Louis Post Dispatch*, was a lot less noble than that. "There was not a lot of structure. It was a messy house. There was a basic lack of organization. The kids basically took over. It's great entertainment for us now as adults to laugh hysterically about what went on in our house. It was crazy. As a child, it was insanity."

One positive effect of growing up amid abject poverty and a large family was that Sarah was extremely unspoiled and generous to a fault. She credited her mother, in particular, for giving her a true sense of the importance of family. "What I gained from my mother is this love," she related in *Redbook*. "She created this environment where the children were allies for each other. I also think she created neurosis in her children but, then, what parent doesn't?"

A big part of this neurosis occurred when Sarah discovered sex. There were no secrets in the Forste house. With four more children arriving at various times in Sarah's youth, the youngster, aided by her older brothers' and sister's insight into the subject, soon discovered sex. "I don't think I learned about sex from my parents," she once said. "But I have seven brothers and sisters, so we had an implicit understanding of where babies come from. When my mother told me she was pregnant with child number seven, I was almost embarrassed because, by then, I was old enough to understand, and the thought of her doing that seven times was just too much for me."

While Sarah got along well with all her siblings, as she grew older she developed a particular admiration for her older sister, Rachel. Whereas Sarah was vain and self-involved as a child, her older sister, in her eyes, was the model of responsibility in and out of the house. Her sister did very well in school, and, in the chaotic household that Sarah grew up in, she would willingly change diapers and bathe and feed the younger children. What impressed Sarah the most was that Rachel did all this and more without complaint. Sarah, with childlike logic, thought that since her sister must have loved everything she did, it was important that she find something that she felt good about doing as well.

While neither Paul nor Barbara had any great involvement in show business (although Paul did work in the technical side of theater from time to time), both thought that it was important that their children have some grounding in the fine arts. Barbara, in later years, would often concede that, while she was not the stereotypical stage mother, she did have a subconscious interest in seeing her children succeed on some level in the arts. Through state-sponsored scholarships and school-sponsored activities, the growing Parker-Forste clan was treated to ballet, music, and theater classes. That the children took to these diversions so readily made practicing at home that much easier, especially when practice traditionally began before dawn. "My school days usually began at

6 a.m.," Sarah told the *Los Angeles Times*. "With eight children in the family, we would have to switch off. Two would practice on the piano, then switch with two others, while others would be playing viola and violin or working out on a staircase bannister that doubled as a ballet bar. I was exhausted by the time I left for school."

Both of Sarah's parents were politically active and took great pains to impart their attitudes to their children. Sarah remembers that the family always seemed to be wearing black armbands for some cause or another. She also recalls the embarrassment of the day the family marched en masse up and down outside a Cincinnati fast-food restaurant, protesting what they perceived as unfair wage and hiring practices. One of Sarah's most prominent childhood memories during the family's rounds of activism is of meeting presidential candidate Senator George McGovern on a whistle-stop tour of Cincinnati in 1972. In hindsight, those moments were therapeutic for Sarah and her brothers and sisters. They brought home the point that there were people who were worse off than they were and that being involved in changing things for the better was a noble cause.

While Sarah and her siblings were always pointed in the direction of the fine arts, in particular symphony, opera, and theater, the constant lack of money prevented them from attending many professional performances. It was a rare and truly special occasion when the entire family could afford to go to the movies. At the other extreme, the children were not allowed to watch television, with one exception. "Growing up, I just assumed that PBS was the only station our television could get," Sarah once said. Which is not to say that, when their parents were out, Sarah and her brothers and sisters did not sneak a look at the tube. But, as she recalled in an interview with *Empire*, her mother always had a way of finding out. "When Mom came home, she used to put her hand on the set," chuckled Sarah. "If it was warm, then her hand went from the set to our faces." Sarah's parents did not think much of the quality of what passed for entertainment in general but, being the socially and culturally aware person she was, Barbara had a particular problem with television, and it was an attitude that would make an indelible impression on her daughter. Sarah told the *Christian Science Monitor*, "The way women, young women, were depicted in shows when I was younger, my mother thought was reprehensible."

But reading was a whole other matter. "That's what we did in our house," Sarah recalled in a *Los Angeles Times* interview. "My mother would tell us to go to bed and we'd hide in the closet, turn the lights on, and read."

Along the way, Sarah began to catalog influences that would serve her well in the years to come. She understood dance and movement and was instinctively drawn to physical comedy. Feeding that desire, the family made a point of scraping together enough money each year to see Marcel Marceau on his annual visit to Cincinnati. Sarah also had a thing for the great ladies of film and song, showing a particular interest in Carole Lombard and Judy Holliday.

The young girl also showed a particular aptitude for ballet and shortly after she turned eight was admitted on a scholarship to the College Conservatory of Music in Cincinnati, where she honed her ballet skills in several full-length ballets and operas. David Blackburn, one of Sarah's teachers, remembered Sarah as an "extremely focused" girl who took even seemingly small roles seriously. An example of her dedication was the school's production of *The Nutcracker*, in which Sarah was cast as a mouse and was required to stand on her head and kick her legs when the clock struck 12. She practiced the scene endlessly at home, every hour on the hour. Her mother was so concerned that she called Mr. Blackburn, worried that her practicing might cause some serious harm.

Despite the theatrical nature of these productions and her obvious skills as a performer, Sarah did not seem to show much interest in acting at that point. Which was fine with her mother, because Barbara was growing uneasy at the prospect of any of her children entering a professional acting career. Coming from a childhood filled with disappointment, the last thing her children needed was to enter a profession that was rife with rejection. Sarah recalled that her mother was always coaxing them in the direction of teaching or something that had to do with reading and writing. "She didn't mind me being in theater arts. But she would have been happier if I had wanted to work in a museum as a curator or something like that." However, as the years went by and Sarah's interest in acting grew, it was an unwritten agreement between mother and daughter that Sarah was definitely heading in an artistic direction that included the possibility of acting. "Although it wasn't like I was looking for a vocation," she explained in an *US* interview. "It was something that, occasionally, got me out of school. When people say you're good at something when you're young, it means a lot to you."

The school productions gave Sarah a measure of individuality that was hard to come by in the crowded Forste household. Despite her misgivings, Barbara believed that her second daughter would make her mark. Her big break came one day when she was reading through the local paper and, in a children's supplement, found an ad for auditions for a local television special based on the timeless children's story *The Little Match Girl* by Hans Christian Andersen. Sarah took the ad to her mother with a surprising request. "I really don't know why [I wanted to audition]," she recalled in a *Redbook* interview. "I had never acted before in my life." In later years, Sarah was more candid about her reason for doing *The Little Match Girl*—to get away from her family. "Going away from the house was great," she told the *St. Louis Post Dispatch*. "They paid me cash, I got away from home and I didn't have to share with any other kids when I was on the set. All these things are great when you're a kid. It was about having something for myself."

When Sarah persisted, Barbara, who had been hesitant at first, was heartened that her daughter was making this important decision on her own. On the audition day, Barbara drove her daughter to the television studio, where they found 500 other girls gathered for the audition. Barbara was nervous about the amount of competition and concerned about what losing out would do to her daughter's confidence and desire. Sarah, on the other hand, was poised and upbeat as she sat waiting for her turn. It quickly became evident that Sarah, because of her diminutive size, expressive personality, and extensive experience in ballet productions, was perfect for the title role. "I was sort of fresh and natural at the time," she speculated in the *Chicago Tribune* about the reason for her selection.

This regional production of *The Little Match Girl* was done by one of the many television production companies that dotted the Midwest and the South. Faced with small budgets but high levels of talent both in front of and behind the camera, they would do specials and low-budget television fare that would air in their local markets and, possibly, get syndicated in other parts of the country.

The Little Match Girl, shot in a mere five days, was an eye-opening experience for the impressionable Sarah. While she admittedly often struggled to pay attention during regular school lessons, she instinctively gravitated toward the disciplines required to create a television program. Sarah was a quick study and surprisingly adept at learning dialogue and performing in front of the camera. While she was prone to giggles and occasional bouts of expected childlike insecurity, those privy to her first professional performance were impressed with her maturity and ability to adjust to the realities of filmmaking. Given her background, Sarah found it easy to identify with the poverty and hardship endured by her character.

That she was being paid $100 a day in her first professional job was almost an afterthought. After all, Sarah was still a child and had different priorities. "They gave me $5 each day and I'd go to McDonald's for a burger, fries, and a coke and then I'd go to Baskin Robbins for an ice cream," she recalled in a *Redbook* interview. "I thought this was the most fantastic life. I couldn't imagine doing anything better."

Sarah's appearance in *The Little Match Girl* brought no small amount of attention to the Forste family. The *Cincinnati Post* newspaper gave Sarah her first publicity when a local television reviewer gushed, "Sarah Parker will tear your heart out by the roots with her wistful, sensitive portrayal." Overnight, Sarah became the neighborhood celebrity. But it was to her credit that all the fuss—including requests for autographs—did not go to her head, although she would later admit that the attention was nice and that it probably, in later years, helped to turn her in the direction of acting.

Sarah's success in *The Little Match Girl* was contagious, and, over the next year, her older brothers, Timothy and Pippen, joined her in blanketing the Cincinnati-area theater scene with their presence. In fact, while the entire family was very close, it was apparent that Sarah and her two older brothers were destined for the spotlight. Barbara and Paul had come around to the idea that maybe acting was not so bad and were totally supportive of their children. It was the rare show that they and a good part of their family did not attend, and, although they were not going ot push any of their children into that high-risk profession, they were not going to discourage them either. They knew acting might just be their children's way out of the cycle of poverty.

The family soon discovered that opportunities in Cincinnati were limited, and, within a year, a regular topic of conversation was that, if Sarah and her siblings were to progress in their chosen field, they would have to go elsewhere. In 1976, Paul spotted a casting call for the Broadway production of *The Innocents*, which is based on Henry James's classic ghost story *The Turn of the Screw*. Encouraged by their local success, the family made the impetuous decision to go to New York for the auditions. Driving to New York was an adventure in itself for the family. During the trip, Barbara, still concerned about rejection, gently warned the children that Broadway was different from Cincinnati and that the competition would be a lot tougher.

Barbara was right. Whereas a lot of the actors in Cincinnati had been amateurs, the children competing for parts in *The Innocents* were largely polished New York professionals, many of whom already had Broadway credits on their résumés. The auditions were highly competitive. The producers were looking for professional actors with an ability to come across to an audience as real people. Sarah was relaxed and confident the day she auditioned, and the producers were impressed. Both she and Timothy landed roles in the play. She would be playing the pivotal role of a possessed young girl. For nine-year-old Sarah, *The Innocents* was a giant step forward.

The Innocents was typical of the shows running on Broadway at the time. It was a time-honored play—a sure bet to sell tickets. And this particular production would have the advantage of a name director and star. Harold Pinter, an internationally renowned playwright and director, was a kind, skillful, and patient presence who nurtured Sarah through the intricacies of the play with a steady hand. She would later recall that she felt very comfortable around him. She was predictably tentative during the rehearsals, but she also proved to be a quick study.

Claire Bloom, one of the leading actresses of her day, recalled in a *Mirabella* conversation that she first became aware of her future costar when Pinter gave her an update on how the auditions were going. "Harold said, 'Well, there's this wonderful girl from New York. We'll bring her over.'" Bloom was suitably impressed with Parker's maturity and manners. And from many years on the Broadway stage, Bloom sensed that Sarah was not the typical child actor. There was a freshness and spontaneity about her that made her immediately stand out. Bloom told Pinter that they need not look any further for her costar.

Although Sarah was working with an established star of Bloom's magnitude and was new to the rigors of playing a challenging role on a nightly basis in a very adult world, she never appeared overwhelmed at the prospect of performing in front of a packed house and was focused on learning her lines and hitting her cues. Oh, there were the expected butterflies on opening night. But by the time *The Innocents* had ended its three-month run, the critically applauded production proved to Sarah that she was, figuratively speaking, home. "This is what I was suited for," she told *Redbook*. "Going to school every morning made me physically ill. At home I had no structure. This [the theater] gave me one." It was the need for structure and, perhaps, the need to break free from her family and to somehow establish her own identity that finally turned Sarah permanently in the direction of acting.

During the run of the play, Sarah remained under the personal and professional tutelage of Bloom, who, as the run progressed, saw something more than just another child actor in the precocious youngster. The pair would often go to upscale restaurants, and Bloom would make sure that Sarah, in her spare moments back-stage, always had something to read. Sarah was enthralled with the attention Bloom was paying to her away from the theater. It was the first time anyone other than her parents had shown this kind of interest in her, and she came to look upon the actress as a surrogate mother. Bloom agreed that she and Sarah did become fast friends during the run of the play and that she did her best to guide the youngster through the potential pitfalls of working in the theater. She recalled, "I felt that it would be in her long-term interest to not become the typical professional child actor and that she would go further if she was just herself."

"She wanted me to be a lady, to be educated," Sarah revealed in a *Buzz* interview. "I guess she felt that cute and bubbly wouldn't work on Broadway." Bloom need not have worried—by the time Sarah joined the cast of *The Innocents*, she had long since matured beyond childhood into an adult frame of mind. Sarah would rarely bemoan this premature loss of childhood and, in those early days, felt excited at the prospect of growing up and getting on with acting. Reviewers were notoriously tough on child actors on Broadway, so it was a surprise when they cited the believability and depth of Sarah's performance.

Her time in *The Innocents* also began Sarah's love affair with New York. The young, impressionable girl was overcome by the majesty and the character of the city. She loved the restaurants, museums, and other cultural attractions that seemed to be every-where in the Big Apple. The limited glimpses she had of the city showed her that it always seemed to be on. Sarah would excitedly tell her parents and siblings of her latest discovery and vowed that, one day, she would move to New York and have a wonderful life.

Barbara and Paul acknowledged their daughter's enthusiasm. Privately, they took her love for the city very seriously, because, with her first successes as an actress, it seemed logical that Sarah would eventually go where the creative action was. And they had to admit that much of it was in New York.

Flushed with Sarah's success in *The Innocents*, Paul and Barbara made the decision to relocate permanently to New York so their children would have the opportunity to do more theater work. The family was excited at the prospect of going to the big city to live, although Barbara felt uneasy over leaving the relatively safe and secure suburban environment and was homesick. "I think the only person who didn't have much enthusiasm [for the move] was my mother," Sarah recalled in *New Woman*. "She gave up a lot to come to New York City."

They settled into a mixed-income housing project called Roosevelt Island. The children were enrolled in local schools, and, not too surprisingly, Sarah continued to struggle. While her siblings had always done well in school, she was easily distracted, and, by this point, academics could not compete with her dreams of being on stage. But given the emphasis on education in the Forste household, there was never a question that Sarah would complete her formal education and, her mother hoped, go on to college.

Despite the recent breakthroughs of their children, the Forste family was still quite destitute. Their poverty was much in evidence, as Sarah reported in the *New York Times*, once the family settled into Roosevelt Island. "There was a sort of a caste system. It was a sliding scale with some subsidized housing. The families with the least money lived in the less desirable apartments. We were in the house closest to the parking lot. And so everybody knew."

Growing Up Sarah   2

Things began to look up. Paul Forste started a moving company for traveling Broadway productions that was bringing in some badly needed money. With 10 mouths to feed, the Forste clan was far from rich, but now they could honestly say that they had taken the first steps out of poverty and toward some semblance of a middle-class life.

By the time the run of *The Innocents* concluded, it was a given that at least four of the Parker-Forste clan (Sarah, Timothy, Pippen, and Megan) were serious about acting and the possibilities in the world of theater—so much so that Paul and Barbara made the decision to move the family out of Roosevelt Island and to the small town of Dobbs Ferry, 20 miles north of Manhattan, where they could afford a larger house but still be fairly close to the Manhattan theater district and any audition possibilities. And the timing could not have been better. New York theater was undergoing a renaissance. After nearly a decade in which major Broadway shows—usually traditional, mainstream, and commercially safe productions—were the sole attraction for theatergoers, interest was switching to Off Broadway and even Off Off Broadway productions, in which experimental and often risky productions were the rule. It seemed that 99-seat theaters were suddenly springing up on every street corner and in every storefront and

At home on stage

loft. The increase in the number of theaters in New York meant more opportunities for actors of all ages.

Sarah's parents, realizing that they knew very little about the business side of show business, began their own on-the-job training. They secured a good agent for their children and began learning about things like résumés and head shots.

Throughout 1977, the acting branch of the Forste-Parker family worked fairly regularly. Sarah, Timothy, and Megan joined the cast of the national touring production of *The Sound of Music*, which featured Shirley Jones, star of films such as *Elmer Gantry* and *The Music Man* and the TV hit series *The Partridge Family*. Productions like this have long been the bread and butter of the touring theater business. Touring with established stars and focusing much of their itineraries on the Midwest and the South, shows like *The Sound of Music* were often the proving grounds for up-and-coming actors as well as solid sources of income for proven veterans. For Sarah and her siblings, it was the perfect opportunity.

And it was definitely something new. Appearing on Broadway

had required a lot of adjustment for Sarah. There were the late nights and the odd eating and sleeping schedules. Going on the road would throw new challenges in her path. She would be up-rooted from her family and, for the two-month tour, have no real home. Barbara and Paul were a bit anxious over their children going on the road but were particularly concerned about how Sarah would take this drastic change in her life. They need not have been. For Sarah, crisscrossing the United States to appear in a different city literally every night was an exhilarating, eye-open-ing experience, one she adjusted to surprisingly well and even embraced. Touring to the youngster was one big party, one that included her brothers and sisters and her mother, who had enthu-siastically joined in as chaperone. A tutor helped the children to keep up with their schoolwork. Coming from a large family aided her day-to-day interaction with the large cast and crew. Her out-going personality made her a cast favorite, as did her maturing talent as a singer and dancer. For Sarah, the show itself was like reading a favorite story over and over again. She knew how it was going to end, but getting there was half the fun.

Sarah came off the road with *The Sound of Music* and into what would be the first of many periodic dry spells. The theater was cyclical for performers in the best of times, and, inevitably, there were seasons when no child actor parts were available. Sarah's agent began pursuing television and movie offers, but even they were slow in coming. But Sarah found a way to fill in the dead time. Through years of instruction by her parents on the importance of speaking clearly, she had also established, by age 10, a reputation as one of the youngest and most in-demand commer-cial voice-over actresses on either coast. In 1984, Sarah described the experience to a *TV Guide* reporter: "I was the TV commercial voice-over queen. I would do the talking for pretty blonde girls who couldn't enunciate." But while the television voice-over work was plentiful and lucrative, Sarah's true passion was always the stage. "I just loved the stage," she recalled in looking back on her formative years in a *New York Times* interview. "It's the most purely terrifying and exhilarating thing in my life. You go out in front of an audience, and there is nothing more masochistic. But what a thrill."

And, as Sarah would readily admit in later years, acting gave her the chance to escape the ongoing chaos that was her family life. Although she did not feel comfortable enough to discuss it until years later, Sarah, beginning in her preteen years, was growing frustrated at having to stand in line for the bathroom and having to settle for hand-me-down clothing. It was cute when she was younger. But Sarah was now looking around at her friends and their lives and was often finding hers lacking by comparison. And the line for the bathroom was not getting any shorter. Since relocating to New York, Barbara and Paul had added two more children to the family. With 10 people under one roof, the result, on a good day, bordered on calamity. Barbara once explained the situation to the *St. Louis Post-Dispatch* this way: "When you have eight kids, the kids take over. It's mayhem."

When not working, Sarah was also attempting to have a normal childhood. Although Barbara and Paul had insisted all along that the most important thing was that their children be children, maintaining a normal childhood was becoming increasingly difficult for the acting members of the family. Auditions and rehearsals regularly disrupted family life. It was becoming more and more rare that the entire family sat down to a meal.

And then there was the matter of schooling. At age 12, Sarah and her acting siblings were enrolled in New York's famed Manhattan Professional Children's School, which offered a balance of real-world academics and courses geared to the life of a young professional actor. By all accounts, Sarah continued to thrive in this environment, becoming, through hard work, a good student but an even better actress. In a *Los Angeles Times* interview, she painted a wildly different picture of her academic abilities. "I was a daydreamer. One of those people whose mouths hang open in class. I did not do well in math. I hated school, really, so thank God I had an outlet [acting] because otherwise, I would have felt like a failure."

Throughout the early stages of her career, Sarah remained

surprisingly normal in the face of her growing success as a performer. She displayed none of the brattiness so common to many child actors and appeared to take what she was doing for a living very much in stride. However, Sarah's parents were ever vigilant when it came to bad behavior. Barbara and Paul knew there was the potential for disaster in a 12 year old's growing up in the rarefied and distracting atmosphere of show business, so they took it upon themselves to make sure that Sarah, as well as their other acting children, lived as normal lives as possible when not working. Paul's business had improved to a point where household finances allowed them to send the children to special schools. Barbara was a strict disciplinarian who would not allow Sarah to get away with displays of ego and temper. She was well aware that the theater could do weird things to children, and she was not going to allow that monster to set foot in her house. Consequently, as Sarah recalled in an interview excerpt from *Current Biography*, her preteen years were excruciatingly normal. "I spent the night in sleeping bags and stole money from my mother's purse. I sold Girl Scout cookies and babysat a lot."

Sarah continued to work in musical revues and local productions of the musicals *By Strouse*, *The Nutcracker*, and *The Firebird*, in which she was applauded as an actress, dancer, and singer mature beyond her years. Sarah, at age 12, was more than capable of taking the next step up the acting ladder. In 1978, the Broadway production of *Annie* was one of the hottest tickets in New York and was always on the lookout for talented child actors to take their places in an ever-evolving cast. Sarah's agent sensed that a part in *Annie*, any part, would be a big career move. And so, when it was announced that the Broadway company was holding auditions for background singers and actors, he advised Sarah to pick out a favorite song and to practice it. On the day of the audition, Sarah reportedly impressed the producers and casting people with a sterling rendition of the song "Nothing" from the musical *A Chorus Line* and was immediately accepted into the cast. For her first year in *Annie*, Sarah's primary role was as one of the orphans in the story. She had few lines, but her bubbly personality made an immediate impression. Her talents as a charismatic, potential star, and the fact that she had taken the time to sharpen her singing skills, were immediately recognized. As she entered her first year with the show, she also took on the mantle of understudy to the reigning Annie, Shelly Bruce.

Sarah's past theater experience served her well in *Annie*. With a cast almost totally populated by children, it was just a bigger version of her own life, so she was able to cope with the pandemonium that inevitably surfaced during rehearsals and backstage just before show time. When Bruce left the show in 1979 (or most likely had outgrown the part of the perennial 11-year-old Annie), Sarah became the third young actress to step into the title role, a part she would play on a nearly nonstop basis for the next two years. She also made her film debut that year, playing the small role of a preteen in the youth-oriented divorce drama *Rich Kids*. While the role itself was largely insignificant, the experience she gained on the movie set was invaluable in opening up the youngster's eyes to a new element of her ever-expanding world.

Sarah's two-year stint in the role of Annie was a roller coaster of emotions. Her obvious talents as an all-around performer were leading to the ego boost of her first rave reviews. She was learning more about the world of theater and reveling in the level of satisfaction that theaters, directors, and other actors brought her. Sarah found comfort in the fact that the theater, much like her home life, did not stand on ceremony. "In the theater, there's a real work ethic," she once told *Empire*. "No one gets you tea or drinks or a chair." She also marveled at the fact that she was making more money than she ever had in her short career. For somebody so young and innocent in so many ways, Sarah became very aware of the power of money. Money was the reason things were not as bad as they used to be at home. Money was why when Christmas came around, they could now count on something being under the tree.

This was also an exciting time for the Parker-Forste family in general. At the same time that Sarah was starring in *Annie*, her sister Megan was appearing around the corner in a production of

Evita, while, a couple of blocks away, her brother Timothy was appearing in the play *Runaways*. When not on stage themselves, the youngsters could usually be found in the audiences of their siblings' performances, and Barbara and Paul would always make appearances at the shows featuring their growing stable of acting children.

But while things were looking up for the Forste family in general, the young star of *Annie* was also coming to grips with the fact that stardom at a young age came with a price. The reality of being a star on Broadway was that Sarah had to give up any semblance of a normal childhood. At a time when she should have been socializing, partying, and perhaps dating, Sarah, at the highly impressionable and volatile age of 13, was living and working in an adult world that saw her performing six shows a week and two on Sunday. And, although Sarah was happy with what she was doing, there were those occasional days when both she and her mother entertained the idea that she might be happier doing something else. Sarah would admit in later years that, despite the notoriety of appearing in one of the most successful plays in Broadway history, there were moments, usually when she was tired or not feeling well, that she wished she could be a normal girl. But then she would hear the applause and her musical intro, and the professional in her would take over.

Barbara often said, "We never wanted Sarah to think acting was more important than pursuing any other career," and she always prodded her daughter to "buckle down in school and attend college." But there was more to these concerns than career and college. Even at that tender age, Sarah was aware that, in terms of her social development, she was severely delayed. "People always thought of me as much younger than I actually was," she said in a *Harper's Bazaar* interview. "You have to remember that from age 12 to 15, I played an 11-year-old every night." Consequently, by the time Sarah left *Annie*, she was experiencing personal and professional insecurities. The stage had literally been her second home for three years, and there was obvious sadness in leaving it. And there was also a real concern that she might have trouble finding other work. "After *Annie*, it was very scary because I'd left a mark which said I was a young girl in a lampshade dress who could sing very loudly and that wasn't me at all." Sarah was also facing a reality that had felled more than one child actor. At age 15, physically and emotionally, she was entering an awkward age. Although she had always played younger roles, casting directors were starting to see her as being slightly too old for preteen parts. The flip side was that Sarah did not yet look old enough to play teen and older parts. She was caught in the middle. But Sarah brought a sense of reality to every part she played. That was something that few actors of any age possessed, and Sarah came by it naturally. If she could hang on through this temporary dip, she would definitely find work.

While starring in *Annie*, Sarah worked nights and slept days, leaving her no time to go to school, but a tutor helped her to keep up with her education. She returned to regular classes at the Manhattan Professional Children's School, where she immediately felt awkward and insecure in the face of real-life challenges such as dating and suddenly having to relate on a daily basis to kids her own age after two years in a world largely populated by adults and professional children. Sarah's typically sparkling, outgoing personality began to retreat into shyness. Her grades took a nosedive. But it was to Sarah's credit that, when she began doing badly in school, she used her own money to hire a private tutor until her grades improved.

Professionally, her success in *Annie* had created a whole different set of problems for Sarah. Her fear of the dreaded stereotype had become a reality. The phone had stopped ringing. "When I left the show at 15, it put a lot of pressure on me to carry on the sort of *Annie* tradition," she revealed to the *Los Angeles Herald Examiner*. "That wasn't a bad thing. I just felt I wasn't equal to what people expected of me. They expected me to audition for a Broadway show and sing so loud I hurt them. I was the only Annie I can think of who didn't have a huge, belting voice."

Sarah's identity crisis was further complicated by normal teenage desires. She often found herself disappointed and angry with the family's continuing financial struggles. When her friends were walking around town in designer jeans or, in some cases, driving brand-new cars, Sarah was still wearing less than stellar clothes, and, with so many mouths to feed and bills to pay, she was, with few exceptions, being denied even the simplest material pleasures. Admittedly, the questions about showbiz kids and their money were complicated by a New York law that was in a state of flux. In those days, there was no legislation requiring that some of a child actor's earnings go directly into a trust. There was also no law declaring how much a child actor could work. Sarah would never have questioned how her parents were spending her money because the needs of the family came first. But looking back on those times in later years, she conceded that, if she had it to do over again, her money would have been handled a bit differently. "If I knew then what I know now, I would have had somebody outside the family help me manage my money," she said candidly in a New York Times interview. "An objective party that would keep things real clean so that, when you're a teenager, you don't feel resentful that you can't at least keep some of it." But she was quick to point out that none of her money, as well as that of her acting siblings, ever went to extravagant things like cars and trips but always to day-to-day living expenses. Knowing that, Sarah could easily abide the situation at that time.

Adding to the normal teenage angst Sarah was experiencing following Annie was the continued lack of work. She came to the mature decision to try a change of pace. Rather than continuing to press for star-level parts, of which there were few for children her age, Sarah joined the decidedly low-profile children's chorus of the Metropolitan Opera. Her reasoning was that, after years of being in the spotlight and the center of attention, "I needed to be one of 25 kids and not be treated specially."

After a season with the Metropolitan Opera, during which she sang and performed in the musical productions Hansel and Gretel, Cavaleria Rusticana, I Pagliacci, and Parade, Sarah was once again at ease and ready to find a job. Happily, she found that during her time with the Metropolitan Opera the impact of Annie had finally worn off, and in the eyes of producers and casting people she was considered a capable young actress but nothing approaching a star. Which was just the way Sarah wanted it.

Her first job after leaving the Met was the small, undistinguished role of a young girl in a better-than-average, made-for-television movie called *My Body, My Child*, a melodrama centering on a woman's decision to either have an abortion or give birth to a deformed child. On that film, Sarah reaped the benefits of working with a talented, experienced cast that included Oscar-winner Vanessa Redgrave (*Julia*, 1978) and veteran Jack Albertson, who had appeared in such classics as *Miracle on 34th Street* (1947) and *The Poseidon Adventure* (1972). This was to be his last project—he died in November of 1981. Also in the cast was her future *Sex and the City* costar Cynthia Nixon, whose credits included *Amadeus* (1984). Sarah received more screen time than she had on *Rich Kids* and came to feel comfortable in front of the camera. But even though she liked the hustle and bustle of a movie set, she missed the theater and wished she could get back on the stage.

Following *My Body, My Child*, Sarah returned to her true love, the theater, and was in active rehearsal for another Broadway-bound play when she was offered a role in a brand-new television series called *Square Pegs*. The show chronicled the misadventures of two klutzy girls who try to worm their way into the in crowd at their high school. While *Square Pegs* seemed to be just the latest in a long line of disposable, mindless television fare, the show, at least on paper, had a lot more going for it. The dialogue and situations rang true, and the leads were both nonstereotypical girls. By television standards, *Square Pegs* was attempting to take a small step forward.

Sarah was facing a dilemma. The purist in her thought that she should stick with the theater. But the realist in her knew that the offer of a television series did not come along very often, and that kind of exposure could do wonders in terms of her career. There was also the concern that her mother would not approve. However, Barbara did not have any problems with the show and

RON GROVER / SHOOTING STAR

Sarah Jessica Parker and Amy Linker in *Square Pegs*

even applauded the fact that *Square Pegs* focused on the trials and tribulations of the average student rather than the jock and the cheerleader. After much hand-wringing, Sarah, then 16, said yes to *Square Pegs*. "I felt I was some kind of traitor," she confessed in a *Herald Examiner* interview. "I thought 'You're so impure, you're selling out.' I thought all my theater friends in New York would think I was a bad person." Sarah's acceptance of the *Square Pegs* role also caused a major change in her family's life. With the show being filmed in Los Angeles, it was decided that Barbara and her two youngest children would accompany Sarah and live there during the filming of the show's first season, while Paul would remain on the east coast with the older children as they continued their school and acting careers. His theatrical moving company was a success but required his attention as well.

Paul and Barbara had finally adjusted to the fact that some of their children were working actors and that concessions would have to be made. As always, the nonacting members of the family were a major consideration in any decision, and those children would often look back on those times without a hint of jealousy or anger.

Sarah's year in Los Angeles put her through a whole new set of experiences. Although she took most of her schooling on the set, Sarah was enrolled as a junior at the famed Hollywood High School. She lived with her mother in an apartment in nearby Toluca Lake and commuted daily to either the nearby North Hollywood studios where much of *Square Pegs* was filmed or the actual high school in Norwalk where many of the exterior scenes were shot. Unlike theater and movies, television was pretty much an unglamorous grind in which her workday would often begin as early as 7 a.m. and could easily go 12 hours. The speed with which the typical television show was shot required Sarah to be a quick study of her lines. "It was like being in the army," she recalled of the exhausting experience.

But the teenager made a surprisingly quick adjustment to working in television and, as the season progressed, proved adept at doing comedy. Critically speaking, *Square Pegs* was a success, and many of the reviewers singled out Sarah and her inherent believability in the role of nerdy freshman Patty Greene as the main reason to tune in to the show. The reality was that, to a large extent, Sarah was not acting. There was much in her upbringing and natural approach to life that made her *Square Pegs* character an extension of her personality. Unfortunately, the good notices for Sarah did not translate into good ratings for *Square Pegs*, and the show was canceled after that first season. It had aired on CBS between September 27, 1982, and September 12, 1983. "Had *Square Pegs* come along two years later, I think it would have been a huge hit," Sarah would tell *Buzz* years later. "But, at the time, it really went against the image of women."

Sarah was disappointed at the cancellation of the show, but, due in large part to the exposure that came with a year on television, the offers began to pour in. Her costars had some success as well. Merritt Butrick appeared in some of the *Star Trek* films; Rick Nelson's daughter Tracy had a career in movies and television;

and Jami Gertz had roles in hit films like *Sixteen Candles* (1984) and *Twister* (1996).

Sarah was catapulted into her first starring role in a movie in a small, offbeat film called *Somewhere Tomorrow*. The film was a drama about a fatherless teen who meets the ghost of a boy who was killed in a plane crash, and it was a proving ground for Sarah. Shot quickly on a small budget, it meant that she had to know her lines and be prepared to carry the film on a number of emotional levels. But her work on *Somewhere Tomorrow* indicated that she was an actress fully capable of projecting warmth and pathos in an adult, nonpreppy way, and, at the young age of 17, she demonstrated that she was more than seasoned enough to carry a film. However, the good notices were more than balanced by her first bout of type casting after *Square Pegs*. "Because of *Square Pegs*, I was viewed as geeky and cerebral," she told the *Chicago Tribune*. "I had been told on several occasions that the truth of the matter was that I wasn't pretty enough to play the pretty girl. It was an endless struggle and a source of great frustration." And no small amount of hurt. No 17 year old wants to be told that she is not pretty. Her parents assured her that she was, in fact, beautiful. Sarah had to admit that her looks did not match the perfect images of leading ladies, but she could console herself with the fact that at least she was working.

For Sarah, the obvious success she was having was not enough, though. There were moments when she continued to long for a more normal life, which she had to admit was sorely lacking. She had never had a steady boyfriend, had barely had a date throughout high school, and when it came to affairs of the heart she was hopelessly naïve.

After finishing the shoot on *Somewhere Tomorrow* in Los Angeles, Sarah returned home to New York, where she entered her senior year in high school. She was seriously considering putting her acting career on hold and going to college. In fact, her grades had improved so much that she could have easily entered many of the most prestigious east coast universities. In particular, Sarah had an eye on Smith College, where she figured she could blend in and see what a regular life had in store for her. But any plans for higher education were put on hold when the offer came for Sarah to go to Los Angeles to audition for a costarring role in the musical drama *Footloose*. It was the kind of movie Hollywood traditionally considered a risky venture. Movies that relied on music and heavy choreography rarely did well. Throw teens into the mix and the odds against success immediately stacked up. But the buzz in Hollywood regarding *Footloose* was very good. This tale of a city boy transplanted to a small Midwest town who fights the town's edict against music and dancing was a big-budget musical that featured a strong list of relative newcomers that included Kevin Bacon, who had shot to stardom just two years earlier with *Diner* (1982); Lori Singer, fresh from her turn on the TV hit series *Fame*; and Chris Penn, who had had a part in the 1983 hit *Rumble Fish*. Most actors would likely have killed for a shot at *Footloose*. But when the film producers wanted her to cut her hair and dye it red, Sarah had an unexpected fit of youthful defiance. The producers' immediate response was to back down and ask Sarah to be in Los Angeles the next morning. "I didn't know whether I should be very presumptuous and pack a big suitcase or pack a little one and have nothing to wear for eight weeks," she laughingly recalled. Fortunately, Sarah packed a large suitcase. She soon found herself on the set of *Footloose*. The music and dance of the film played to her strengths, and in the eyes of her fellow performers and the filmmakers she had, by age 19, matured into a well-rounded, talented performer.

For the first time, Sarah was in a cast made up primarily of her peers, and she fit easily into the party atmosphere. There were pool parties and barbecues. And teen-magazine reporters came on set, snapped pictures, and interviewed the stars of the film. Sarah broke into peals of laughter when her face first appeared in *Sixteen Magazine*. She thought the idea of being in the public eye was hilarious.

It was on the set of *Footloose* that Sarah finally grew up. Chris Penn (Sean's brother) was six years older than Sarah. He was out-

Fooling around in New York City's Central Park in 1984

going, seemingly sensitive, and very handsome. She was always nervous around him. She did not have enough experience to know whether she was feeling love or lust. Whatever it was, Penn felt it too, and the pair were soon involved in a romance in which she lost her virginity. Like most such romances, the relationship between Sarah and Chris had cooled by the time *Footloose* completed filming. She would look back in later years on her first serious sexual relationship with mixed emotions, but she was surprisingly evenhanded in assessing the end of her first romance. "When you're young or when you first have sex, it's not necessarily enjoyed," she told a *Playboy* interviewer. "My first time, I didn't know enough about myself and I didn't know enough about sex. I was way older than most people are. I was at the point of no return, where you can't ask questions." She joked that it was surprising that she had remained a virgin that long.

Footloose would remain a pivotal moment in her life. She emerged from the experience a woman, and, once the reviews started coming in, many of which recognized her talent and promise despite the fact that she was not one of the top-line performers, the consensus was that she was now a star in the making. Sarah, after spending years wondering whether to commit to a full-time acting career, was starting to believe it was possible. In her mind, there was now no other option. She was an actress.

Sarah returned to New York after the completion of *Footloose*. Her confidence knew no bounds. She had grown up as an actress and a woman. Sarah was very much her own person and, as such, had developed an independent streak, one that precluded her from returning to the crowded Forste household.

Paul and Barbara noticed the change and thought that their daughter was old enough to make her own decisions. Consequently, they did not put up much of a fight when Sarah announced that she was moving out on her own. She found a small apartment in New York, and, on that first night in her new place, she was deliriously happy at just being alone.

Down with Downey  3

The first time Sarah Jessica Parker saw Robert Downey Jr. on the set of the film *Firstborn*, nobody would have blamed her if she had run the other way. Downey, outfitted in a spiky punk hairdo and glasses decorated with Superman stickers, looked downright scary. "I guess Sarah thought I looked scary enough to be interesting," Downey remembered in a *People* magazine interview. Not exactly. As it turned out, what Sarah saw in the wiry 19-year-old actor was a soulful personality that radiated humanity and tenderness from his puppy dog eyes. She could not take her eyes off him. Downey, looking back on that moment in a *Mirabella* interview, couched his memories in near-spiritual terms. "She was sitting across the room and I thought, 'You have a lot to learn from this person.'"

Sarah and Downey had a lot in common. Both had come from large, fragmented, nontraditional, artsy families. They had both entered show business at a very early age, and they were both still essentially children who tended to look at life in a rather simplistic way. And, like Sarah, Downey was slowly but surely crawling up the Hollywood ladder with good notices in films like John Sayles's *Baby, It's You* (1983).

But there was also much that was different. Sarah had been raised in a rather conservative environment that precluded her experimentation with sex, drugs, and alcohol. No one would ever mistake her for a party girl. Downey, however, at a relatively early age, was the epitome of overindulgence. It was not uncommon for the young actor to be out all night and not remember the next morning where he'd been. Friends and associates alike were often forthcoming in stating that there was a self-destructive streak buried not too deeply inside the actor. He was also known to be quite the ladies' man, having had a string of short but intense relationships. In contrast, Sarah was an icon of purity and innocence. It was the classic case of opposites attracting. On a subconscious level, Sarah was perhaps attracted to his unpredictability. Downey was nothing like any male figure who had been in her life. It was obvious that he was everything she was not. All she knew was that she was incredibly attracted to him.

Sarah made a point of getting to know her young costar. She had heard all the stories. Brought up in a fractured filmmaking family and already wise beyond his years in the ways of alcohol, drugs, and sex, on the surface Downey did not seem to be a good risk when it came to entering a romantic relationship. The young woman was sure that her parents would not approve. But Sarah, an incurable romantic, chose to ignore his shady past and saw Downey, in his punk rock outfit on the set of *Firstborn*, as Prince Charming. "Downey was so grand," she once gushed to *Redbook*. "His lifestyle was like fancy cars and big houses." For his part, Downey was instantly attracted to Sarah. Her physical beauty was obvious to him. Her bright spirit and positive outlook, qualities he was not used to finding in his circle of friends, were exceedingly attractive. And, unlike a number of previous partners, Sarah seemed to be interested in who he was rather than in his potential. "He's a combination of apple pie and Jack Kerouac," she once told *Model* in looking back on her initial impressions of Downey. "Robert's not the maniac people think he is, but he's not quiet either. He's very complex, interesting, and dangerous. He's just sort of unpredictable." And after a life that had been, up to then, rather safe and conservative, she was ready for somebody who would constantly test the boundaries of convention and take her along for the ride.

In the early days of production for *Firstborn*, the pair did a cautious mating dance. The chemistry in their scenes together was good. But off camera, there was an equal amount of nervousness as they talked around their true feelings and waited for the other to make the first move. Finally, Sarah made that move herself. At the time, she was working in *Firstborn* during the day and, at night, acting on Broadway in the play *To Gillian on Her 37th Birthday*. One day on the *Firstborn* set, Sarah approached Downey and asked him if he would meet her at the theater after the show. Sarah shocked herself with her own boldness. Being that forward was not even remotely part of her makeup. She was even more shocked when Downey readily agreed to meet her. For the rest of that day and at her night job on *To Gillian*, Sarah had a hard time concentrating. She could not wait to meet Downey, although she did not want to be too obvious and make him think she was easy. On the other hand, she did not want to play any teen games either. When they met after the show, Sarah and Downey laid out their feelings: each had been immediately drawn to the other. That night, they were in each other's arms. Within a matter of days, Downey had moved into Sarah's apartment. He reflected on his feelings at the early stages of his relationship with Sarah when he told *Mirabella*, "We were both young and we found each other in all this insanity, and we were trying to play house."

Telling her parents, and particularly Barbara, about her situation left Sarah in a quandary. Did she want to tell her right away or give the relationship some time to see if it was going to work first before breaking it to her mother? One thing weighing in favor of telling Barbara was that she had always been a progressive thinker. Sarah figured that the worst-case scenario that she had concocted in her head would likely not come to pass. So, she made the decision and picked up the phone. At first, Barbara was shocked, surprised, and, perhaps, a little disappointed in her daughter. But in the end, she did what any mother would do—wish her daughter luck and tell her to be careful.

The beginning of Sarah and Downey's relationship was so spontaneous and impetuous that the couple were embarrassed at the prospect of anybody they knew, especially those on the movie *Firstborn*, finding out. The last thing they needed was to be the subject of whispers and gossip. And so, for the remainder of the shoot, while they would take the same cab to the set, Sarah would get out 100 yards ahead of Downey so they would not be seen arriving together. At the end of the day, they would reverse the process. But there was no way Sarah and Downey were going to keep the secret for too long. It would be tough to be around each other on a movie set and not give off an easily discernible vibe. By the time filming wrapped on *Firstborn*, Sarah and Downey's romance was common knowledge and the subject of a lot of good-natured ribbing from the cast and crew.

The couple were still at that starry-eyed stage of their relationship when, six weeks after they met, they were forced to make an important decision. After the completion of *Firstborn*, Downey was immediately offered a film role in Los Angeles, while Sarah, following her successful run on *To Gillian on Her 37th Birthday*, landed a part in a television special in New York. Sarah was not happy at the prospect of being away from Downey. She was concerned, given Downey's reputation, that the time apart would put too much temptation in his path. "It was difficult," she recalled in *People*. "But I wasn't going to say to someone I'd known for six weeks, 'Give up the movie!'" Her faith that Downey would remain faithful was rewarded. During his time in Los Angeles, they were on the phone to each other daily, and, although neither of them would come out and say it, the relationship was beginning to feel like love.

In the coming months, the couple continued an often tentative feeling-out process. Following that first trip to Los Angeles, Sarah became more comfortable with the idea that Downey sometimes had to leave town to work. Likewise, Downey was at ease with the idea that Sarah might not be home every night. When they were not working, they discovered new facets of each other's personality. There were adjustments to be made on both sides. Sarah had grown up in a large family and had only recently gotten used to the idea of living alone. Now she had to get used to living with a man. For Downey, easily the more experienced in affairs of the heart, there was the task of learning to accept love with no strings attached.

Within the year, because of their increasing demand in Hollywood and the fact that Sarah lost the lease on their New York apartment, the couple decided to move permanently to Los Angeles and into a two-story Hollywood carriage house, formerly occupied, over the years, by such diverse personalities as Bette Davis and John Lennon. "We were both big New York advocates," she explained to the *Los Angeles Times*. "It was a difficult decision. I'm a real purist about the theater and that whole thing and believed that no place was better [than New York]." However, Sarah soon found that there was a lot to like in the larger-than-life fantasyland sprawl that was Hollywood. There were places where she could bike ride, roller-skate, and do all the things she used to do in New York. There were restaurants that never closed. Primarily through Downey, she made friends with others in the business. And best of all, she and Downey were together in a relationship that seemed to be growing stronger by the minute.

Although they were lovers, Downey and Sarah were also determined to keep the relationship on a practical level. The couple agreed to split the monthly rent as well as all of the household expenses. Those first few years in Hollywood were a joyous time for Sarah and Downey. Both had begun to move along in their careers, were working regularly, and, despite the high mortality rate among Hollywood couples, continued to present a loving and united front. "We literally grew up together," Sarah once told *Cosmopolitan*. "We love one another and we want to be together." Downey, who had often commented in the past about how he was not ready to settle down, now changed his tune in the face of Sarah's love and devotion. "I'm really starting to gain an understanding of what a relationship is. The shifting of two people into a third thing, not me, not you, but us."

While Downey did not completely cut out his partying ways, there was a noticeable lessening of his indulgences. Although Sarah could never be 100% sure that he had completely given up drugs and booze, and the word among his acquaintances at the time was that he had not, Downey seemed to be committed to toning down his carousing. Sarah was happy for that because, while she had been tolerant of his vices and was still attracted to what she termed "his unpredictability," she had already had glimpses of how helpless and needy he could become when he overindulged. And the last thing Sarah wanted was to end up being a mother figure in her man's life.

Parents always play a role in any relationship, and Sarah and Downey's was no different. Downey's father, Robert Downey Sr., a noted filmmaker, was thrilled that his son finally seemed to be settling down. "I thank God for Sarah Jessica Parker," he once said. "Without her, Robert would go at 100 miles an hour into a brick wall." Barbara, on the other hand, was cautious. She had not been happy with the news that her daughter had chosen to cohabit with a man without the benefit of marriage, and she was occasionally uneasy at the prospect of her daughter living with him in potentially corrupting Hollywood. She thought Downey was a bright, interesting, and generous person, but she was uncomfortable with the fact that they had become so serious at such a young age. In particular, she wished her daughter had tried different relationships before tying herself down. However, she knew better than to argue with her headstrong daughter. So, at the end of the day, all she could offer Sarah was some sage, real-world advice. "The only thing my mother ever said to me was 'Don't forget there's Planned Parenthood in every city,'" she laughed in US.

When it came to children, Barbara need not have worried. Sarah and Downey realized that they were too young and that their careers were too uncertain to start a family, although Sarah, during this period, made it plain that she did want to have a family at some point. On the surface, Barbara's fears appeared to be unfounded because, while barely into their 20s and still very much children at heart, they seemed to be quite good for each other. Always practical when it came to money, Sarah insisted that the normally spendthrift Downey open a banking account and hire an accountant to manage his funds. Downey was quick to credit his relationship with Sarah with dampening his insecurities and raising his self-image as a good person and as a Hollywood actor. The latter statement was not mere hyperbole, for once they moved to Hollywood the young actor was suddenly very much in demand. Throughout the first years of their relationship, Downey was busy, appearing in 1985 alone in the films *Tuff Turf*, *Weird Science*, and *To Live and Die in L.A.*

For Sarah, having Downey in her life salved her insecurities about her own self-image and settled a number of trust issues: one big one was the question of separation. She had never quite gotten over the heartache of her father walking out the door when she was a baby, and she could never quite put the fear out of her mind that it would be an ongoing pattern in her life. That is, not until she met Downey, whose loyalty to her and her needs had succeeded in putting her in a more comfortable and trusting state of mind. It was a good thing, too, because not long after they moved into their Hollywood home the couple landed film assignments that resulted in their being apart for three months. Sarah agreed with Downey's notion that, at that point, their first priority had to be their careers; otherwise, they wouldn't be any good to each other. The separation was a true test of their relationship, one that they happily passed.

With his background as a wild party guy, onlookers were surprised at how quickly Downey slipped into being a remarkable picture of domesticity. Downey and Sarah rarely went to Hollywood parties and movie premieres, preferring quiet nights at home. They thought secure enough in their love that they would often laugh for hours as they bounced the names of children off each other and made hypothetical marriage plans. Hypothetical because, while they felt that marriage was a definite goal in their relationship, they did not want to ruin what they had by planning too far ahead. They were having too much fun jogging, playing on water slides, and dropping water balloons on their neighbors to even think about making adult plans. And who could blame them? Hollywood was a heady place to be for an actor, especially one who was managing to make a success of it. So, they reasoned, why not enjoy it to its fullest?

The media eventually caught wind of Downey and Sarah's relationship and showered them with labels that were variations on Hollywood's New Hot Couple. *People* magazine and other influential periodicals ran at-home pictorials of the couple, and Downey and Sarah did a number of interviews centered on their fairy-tale romance. Downey was the obvious hook, but he was generous in giving Sarah much of the story to tell. She had done some minor press before, but she took enthusiastically to the process of doing interviews and posing for pictures. For Downey, being with Sarah and being successful made the perfect equation according to a *Playboy* interview in which he looked back over his life. "I was making tons of money. I was set up in a relationship with Sarah Jessica Parker. It just seemed like I could do no wrong."

For the first few years of their relationship, it was almost too good to be true. Downey continued to be a top Hollywood draw and had moved up to leading-man status in the films *Less than Zero*, *The Pick Up Artist*, and *True Believer*. Sarah, for her part, was beginning to capture Hollywood's attention on the strength of her performances in the film *Girls Just Want to Have Fun* and a number of well-regarded movies for television.

But eventually the old demons returned to trouble Downey and, by association, Sarah. Downey began to stay out late, sometimes all night, and the look on his face when he did stagger in made it clear that he was once again drinking and doing drugs. Sarah had sensed, even in the most serene times together, that her lover was "one of those tortured souls." And in the back of her mind, she always knew there was the possibility of old habits resurfacing. But in the face of his now obvious backsliding into his addictions, she was at a loss about what to do. "I'd never seen cocaine in my life, and my boyfriend was addicted to it," she sighed as she recalled the emotional pain in a *Redbook* interview. "Having no experience in that world of drugs and having very little understanding of why you just can't give it up if you know it's so destructive." Sarah cajoled, yelled, cried, and did just about anything she could think of to get Downey to stop his substance abuse. For a while, he would get straight, then relapse, then get straight again in a seemingly never-ending vicious cycle. Sarah endured Downey's attempts to kick the habit in a variety of ways, including several well-publicized stints in rehabilitation centers, numerous interventions by family and friends, the periods when he was clean and she would get her hopes up, and the inevitable disappointments when he would once again give in to the temptation of drugs.

Downey, in retrospect, said "It was a nightmare" when describing his time in drug hell. Part of the nightmare was that, while Sarah and Downey were making very good money at the time, most of his was disappearing into the hands of a drug dealer. Downey remembered in a candid and ironic interview with *Details* those tough times when Sarah was essentially supporting them both. "The running joke when I was with Sarah Jessica, she would say 'You just made more money in your last six weeks than I've made in my whole career, and yet I have more money and you're broke and asking me for five grand. What are you doing?' I'd say, 'I don't know. I'll check the trunk. I'm sure there's a bag of something or other that will explain it.'" But as Sarah would attest, Downey's self-destructive drug habit was no joke. As his addiction continued, Sarah retreated into an emotional shell. She would offer up silent prayers when Downey walked out the door, would retire to a quiet corner of their home, and would lose herself in a book or sit quietly in front of the tube, her mind going blank as she watched CNN or a mindless sitcom. With Downey's renewed problems, Sarah began to resent things that had seemingly never been concerns before. One of her biggest peeves became the difference in how their respective careers were going. While Sarah had worked fairly consistently during the years of their relationship, Downey had moved quickly up the Hollywood ladder and was getting more substantial roles in higher-profile films. Consequently, within their Hollywood circle, Sarah had become a lesser entity in the relationship and, more often than not, was introduced at parties as Robert Downey Jr.'s girlfriend.

The romantic vision of Downey was melting away. The rebellious, bad-boy image, which Sarah found attractive when they first met, had now been replaced by a true sense of frustration and pity toward her lover. Sarah could only watch helplessly as the love began to disappear from their lives. Downey's unpredictability had gone from being a turn-on to a curse. Sarah's mother was equally upset and concerned as she watched her daughter's agony and what Downey's addiction was doing to her. Sarah would call her mother regularly and tearfully. Barbara could sense the emotional toll Downey's addiction was taking on her daughter. "I think she spent a lot of time worrying about him," Barbara explained to *Entertainment Weekly*. "In her early 20s, when some girls still want a man to take care of them, she felt responsible for him."

Jill Matson, Sarah's personal assistant at the time, had a front-row seat to the dissolving relationship and recalled that it was not a pretty sight. "She helped him with interventions, you name it," she told *People*. "But you go through a lot with that, lies, deceit, mistrust." In the meantime, Sarah found her normally sunny and positive personality severely tested as she struggled to find the love in a relationship that was rapidly in decline. She began viewing her time when she was working as a refuge from the turmoil surrounding Downey. But, inevitably, her thoughts would return to his suffering and hers. "I just found it incredibly difficult to deal with," she explained to *Redbook*. "You start out worried and sympathetic and understanding, and then you turn angry and bitter and resentful and not particularly loving. It's terrible. You feel so impotent. You're always wondering and waiting for a call from someone saying 'We went to his trailer to get him and he's dead.'"

As the years went on, the couple began to grow in different directions. At the start of their relationship, both admitted that they were essentially still children and that they were growing up together. But as the late 1980s slipped into the 1990s, Sarah's attitude had changed. She was no longer the wide-eyed innocent,

RALPH DOMINGUEZ / GLOBE PHOTOS

Robert Downey Jr. and Sarah

and Downey was no longer the knight in shining armor. "He's just too crazy," she once said in a W interview. "I just grew up."

But the couple fought against Downey's addiction with every ounce of conviction they could muster. After his latest trip to rehab in 1990, Downey was once again in a good place. He would often comment in interviews during this period that his dishonesty and dependence were slipping away. Sarah once again saw glimpses of the person she had fallen in love with in little ways— the way he remembered their anniversary and the pet names he used for her. It was during this period of introspection and candor that Downey told a *Sassy* interviewer, in his own roundabout way, the depth of his feelings for Sarah: "Sarah is my best friend. If I could have something that she has it would be dedication, severe dedication. And to look as good as she does would be nice. I'd love to have her eyes but it's nice just to have them to look at."

But Downey continued to fight a losing battle with his excesses. He would eventually fall back into a life of drugs, alcohol, and nonstop partying with a bunch of faceless hangers-on. By this time, Sarah definitely had leaving Downey on her mind. But there was still a feeling of love for his decent side that made her stay on when he was at his worst. Finally, in 1991, Downey had once again straightened himself out. "I felt so sad," she confessed to *Redbook*, "and by the end, I felt exhausted."

Sarah left Downey in 1991 and returned to New York, where she found a new apartment and began to put her relationship with him behind her. In the end, it was an easy, albeit sad, decision to make. There was nothing she could do for him but watch as he destroyed himself. And she was simply not ready to do that. Downey accepted the blame for Sarah's pain. "I was dishonest with her," he confessed in the aftermath of the breakup. "I blame myself for the split."

In the days and weeks following her decision to move out of their house, Sarah suffered the expected pangs of guilt at the fact that she could do nothing to stop her lover's downward spiral. There were moments when anger consumed her because his vices were finally more important than their love. Theirs had been a high-profile Hollywood relationship, which, at its worst, had already been played out in the press. Her friends and family had known all along what was going on, so rehashing the story with them was not going to be a chore. And those closest to Sarah were relieved that the breakup had been clean and that she had not picked up any of Downey's bad habits along the way.

Through time and reflection, Sarah began to look at her seven years with Downey in a more positive light. She was still troubled by their ultimate inability to commit on a permanent basis. Subconsciously, she vowed never to make that mistake again. In the end, she recalled in an interview with the *St. Louis Post-Dispatch* that "It was time well spent."

Sarah was adjusting just fine to life in the big city. Her already considerable circle of friends cultivated from her theater days was growing. Contrary to her fears, she had been forgiven for doing *Square Pegs*, and she was being hailed as a minor celebrity for her work in *Footloose*. But while she had enjoyed the filmmaking process and knew that Hollywood rather than Broadway would be the place where she would do the majority of her work, she was overjoyed to be back in New York. Her senses were alive with the natural beat of the city and the joy of being young and single in a city that never sleeps.

By 1984, Sarah had already developed an uncanny knack for molding her talents to fit almost any character type, with her somewhat unconventional looks allowing her to play younger and older characters. And so, despite the good notices on *Footloose*, typecasting continued to thwart her chances at playing the Holly-wood leading lady, but she was more than compensated by a myriad of acting challenges that often saw the young actress work-ing in excess.

Shortly after returning to New York, Sarah happily returned to her first love, the stage, in an Off Broadway production of *To Gillian on Her 37th Birthday*. The play, written by Michael Brady, has been a perennial favorite on the big-city theater circuit and has received numerous awards. Sarah was grateful that the role allowed her to move beyond the expected young-girl turns, and she felt herself quite the mature actress on opening night. In a naturalistic approach that would become her trademark, Sarah gave the role of Rachel a genuine quality that quashed the prevailing attitude that all teenagers are precocious. But she knew that it would be the all-important opening-night reviews that would validate her own feelings about her maturing skills as an actress. She survived the expected first-night jitters and delivered a polished performance once the curtain went up. After putting in an appearance at the obligatory premiere party, she raced to a nearby newsstand to await the arrival of the *New York Times* and that all-important first review. "I was at a newsstand at 72nd and Broadway at one in the morning and I screamed when I saw the review," she related in the *Los Angeles Herald Examiner*. "It called me a stage actress, and it was like the best thing I've ever heard about anything in my life. I screamed so loud a policeman came over and asked me if I was okay."

The dichotomy between Sarah the stage actress and the perception Hollywood had of the young performer came crashing through the next morning when she reported to the set of the film *Firstborn*, a drama centering on a divorced woman who inadvertently falls in love with a cocaine dealer. When the part of another supportive girlfriend—not unlike her part in *Footloose*—came up, Sarah was initially not sure she could take it on. Doing a play at night and a movie during the day would be a lot of work, but Sarah figured that she was young and could easily get by on a few hours of sleep and a lot of coffee. The director, Michael Apted, had a good track record with hits such as *Coal Miner's Daughter* (1980); he was a solid presence, and the cast eschewed the perceived B-movie feel. For Sarah, the role of the girlfriend in *Firstborn* was slight, and her dialogue consisted largely of variations on "What's wrong?" in scenes with her live-in love, Robert Downey Jr. Making the decision to be aggressive in her pursuit of Downey's affections had been tough enough for Sarah. Adding to her angst was having to once again adjust to living with another person. Downey was sloppy, while Sarah was meticulous. And the couple had many cap-off-the-toothpaste discussions. But when you're in love, you learn to compromise, and she soon found herself fulfilled with a man in her life and under her roof and a career that was already showing signs of taking off.

These were exciting times for Sarah. She was a young, working, professional actor who was making a life for herself in the big city. Downey's enthusiasm for life and his bohemian attitudes were contagious, and Sarah suddenly found herself experiencing an almost Zen-like appreciation for even the most mundane things in her life. The spartan lifestyle of coffee, cigarettes, and little sleep found a willing adherent in Sarah.

Firstborn was only a modest critical and box office success, but Sarah received generous praise from reviewers that hinted that she was capable of so much more. She followed up the film with a starring role in a television after-school special called *Almost Royal Family*, a slight story about the comic misadventures of a family that inherits an island claimed by both the United States and Canada. This part reinforced the Hollywood perception of Sarah as the perky girl without a care in the world. However, she managed to invest the stock character with some real spirit and substance that transcended the predictable nature of the piece.

Having turned 20, but more than capable of passing for a teen-ager, Sarah was not too surprised when many of the scripts sent her way in the wake of *Firstborn* were the vapid teen comedies that had become a staple in the 1980s. Most of the scripts were blatantly sexist, crude, and just plain bad variations on a tired B-movie template in which the guy chases the girl and finally gets her. These offers she dismissed out of hand, especially those that required nudity. Sarah had long ago vowed she would never do these types of roles.

But one script, *Girls Just Want to Have Fun*, seemed to stand above the rest. Based loosely on the hit single by pop singer Cyndi Lauper, *Girls Just Want to Have Fun* told the story of two girls and their determination to end up as dancers on the TV dance show *American Bandstand*. On the surface, the film was a simple girls-and-guys piece of fluff, but Sarah was immediately attracted by the fact that the central characters were not the dumb and submissive ciphers who normally populate hormonally driven teen films. Rather, they were bright, funny, and witty in an unpatronizing manner. And they seemed to have a realistic outlook on life. This came as no surprise when Sarah discovered that the script had been written by Janis Hirsch, one of the writers on *Square Pegs*, whom Sarah could regularly count on to invest her character of Patty Greene with believable spunk and spirit. But the deciding factor was the opportunity to play the lead in a theatrical film and, hopefully, use it as a stepping stone to more substantial parts. That Sarah was looking at the big picture should come as no surprise. By the time Sarah had landed the lead in *Annie*, she was already thinking of a long-term career, which she logically assumed would climax with her ascending the Hollywood ladder to celebrity and stardom. And, although she was fixated on getting there by good work in quality productions, she knew that those with the power to make and break careers looked at an actor's choices and progress. Consequently, Sarah looked at *Girls Just Want to Have Fun* as much more than just another job. She was looking at it as the next step up.

Sarah's natural style in front of the camera made her the logical choice for the film, and, in fact, Sarah was the first one to be cast. She was happily surprised that one of her new Hollywood friends, actress Helen Hunt, had been picked as her costar. The two young women clicked immediately, sharing experiences of their acting childhoods. Their friendship grew, and the vibe on the set was as light and tension-free as the tone of the film. And Sarah was happy to be given the rare opportunity to project an attractive and sexy image.

Granted, *Girls Just Want to Have Fun* was not great art, but it marked an all-important evolution in Sarah's career. Yes, Sarah was playing a type, but, thanks in large part to the script and direction, she was playing a well-rounded, intelligent character that, like the film itself, managed to overcome the conventions of the teen genre to make a statement about persistence and desire. Sarah's acting style at this point was raw and, to a degree, undisciplined. But, in her first starring role in a commercial, mainstream film, it definitely made an impression. Reviewers tended to fall back on the clichés of "perky" and "spunky" in their takes on the film but indicated that Sarah had invested her character with exactly the right amount of wit and intelligence to lift the role and the film above the predictability of the usual teen flick. The *Los Angeles Times* said that "Parker has the innocent, slightly flustered air of a girl just discovering her budding beauty," while the *Hollywood Reporter* called her "both charming and gawky, graceful and athletic."

Admittedly, a key to Sarah's success in *Girls Just Want to Have Fun* was director Alan Metter's attention to the pulse of the film and its actors. Metter knew what the obvious choices were and studiously avoided them, encouraging Sarah and the other actors to explore other options and to do what came naturally to them. And as Sarah would discover throughout the course of her career, she did her best work under the guidance of directors who pushed their actors in exploring their craft.

In the wake of her success in *Girls Just Want to Have Fun*, Sarah was expecting more mainstream film offers. But the studios remained stubbornly tentative, not knowing what to do with the young actor. Sarah thought she needed to constantly work to improve her skills, so she made it clear that she was available for just about anything. She was next cast in a television biopic on the life and times of Olympic ski champion Billy Johnson, *Going for the Gold: The Billy Johnson Story*. It was a small step forward in which Sarah was once again cast as the supportive girlfriend. The film, which included cast members such as future *ER* hunk Anthony Edwards and soap opera stud Wayne Northrop, got Sarah into some snowy California locales and offered further insights into what it took to turn out a movie for television in a matter of weeks. In the end, the film was pretty much a movie of the week, but it was the kind of exposure Sarah thought she needed to broaden her base in Hollywood.

But her love of the theater was never too far away, and, when she found nothing of interest after completing *Going for the Gold*, she returned to New York, where she appeared for a time in the play *Marathon '86*. The play was a rather low-profile affair, but it served to sharpen and reinforce her strengths as a live performer, as well as make her realize how much she missed being in Downey's arms.

That year, Sarah returned to Hollywood, where she worked with a 12-year-old star, David Freeman, and some time-traveling aliens in a science fiction film tailored largely for preteens entitled *Flight of the Navigator*. She learned how to play off special effects, a skill that would come into play in later years.

Despite the fact that Sarah was not always satisfied with the depth of the parts she was being offered, she had, by 1986, built a reputation and an impressive résumé that showcased her as one of the most naturally gifted, albeit unheralded, actresses around. But praise for her acting talents salved only part of the actress's ego. Roles designed to show her as a sexy and attractive character were still missing. Sarah remained quietly confident that Hollywood's attitude toward her would change, but she confessed to *Buzz* that she would be lying if she said this subconscious neglect of the woman in her did not get to her once in a while. "You know, even if you're a really together person, it's hard not to let other people's opinions affect me. For a long time, it was a real problem for me." But it would not be for long.

In 1986, NBC was in the process of casting a multigenerational saga about the Gardner family of Seattle called *A Year in the Life*. It was ambitious, with strong writing, solid stories, and believable characters. It rejected the expected soap opera clichés that had come to populate nighttime television. The proposed three-part miniseries, created and scripted by Joshua Brand and John Falsey of *St. Elsewhere*, would be directed by up-and-coming young director Thomas Carter, who had been an actor in the cult TV series *The White Shadow* before turning his talents to directing. Sarah heard of the miniseries and wrangled an audition for the part of the young and sexy Kay Ericson. Given her *Square Pegs* baggage — Hollywood tended to label her as the nerdy, not particularly attractive friend — Sarah knew it was a long shot and mentally prepared herself for rejection. But she turned in what she thought was a solid audition. Even so, Sarah was admittedly surprised when she received the call from the producers saying that Carter had loved her audition and wanted her for the role of Kay in *A Year in the Life*. Sarah was grateful to finally have the opportunity to show her attractive side. The miniseries—which included cast members such as veteran actors Richard Kiley and Diana Muldaur and up-and-comers Adam Arkin and Morgan Stevens—was filmed early in 1986, and Sarah blossomed in the role of Kay. That she could be sexy in a sultry way had never been a question for her, but under Carter's free-flowing direction her instincts took over, and she was able to invest Kay with a natural attractiveness that was the perfect level for the character and the show. *A Year in the Life* aired in December 1986 to excellent reviews and high ratings. Sarah's "coming out" was singled out by many critics as a wonderful surprise.

Sarah immediately jumped into another project. *The Room Upstairs* was a standard made-for-television mystery movie in which she turned in yet another solid but not duly heralded performance. But she was already hearing the rumor that NBC had been so pleased with *A Year in the Life* that it was considering spinning it off into a one-hour weekly series. For a number of reasons, Sarah was thrilled when the rumor became a reality and the show was slotted in for the fall 1987 season. The money would obviously be good—more than she had seen in her entire career. But, more importantly, there was the security of a good year's regular work. And finally, with the reality of her progressively shaky life with Downey, a series would give the 22-year-old actress something to keep her mind occupied.

A Year in the Life's evolution from miniseries to weekly series resulted in a change in Sarah's role. Her character, rather than being young and single, was now Kay Ericson Gardner, the new wife of the family's youngest son. Sarah was actually grateful for the change in character because, with the role of wife, she could now leave the teen roles behind and look forward to more mature offerings in the future. During the nearly year-long filming of

Sarah way back in 1986

A Year in the Life, Sarah found herself continuing to grow as an actress. Her natural style was now being supplemented by increased attention to detail brought on by the reality of the long television grind and the fact that they literally had to turn out an hour-long episode in five working days. Sarah thrived in the often nerve-wracking atmosphere and drew praise from her fellow actors and the directors for always being on time and knowing her lines, requirements she had long taken for granted. That she managed over the run of the show to turn Kay into one of the most consistently enticing characters was a tribute to her talent and hard work. When questioned about the superior quality of the show, Sarah was inevitably generous with her praise for the writers. "Show me a feature film that's written as well as that," she said in praising the show to the *New York Times*. "There were no passive or stupid women on that show." And that was the key to Sarah's performance in the series. Her character was smart, intense, and fully realized. This was a liberating time for the actor, her confidence growing as she discovered that she could, in fact, grow beyond the typecasting and show her versatility. And, oh yes, be sexy.

Sarah knew that she had arrived at some level of celebrity when the magazines began printing articles about her, proclaiming her as the Next Big Thing. In interviews, her spirited, enthusiastic side always come through, and when the inevitable questions about her rough childhood arose, she would answer in an honest, direct manner. Predictably, everybody wanted to know about her relationship with Downey, and she was forthright in telling that story, although she always edited out details about his drug problems and their effects on her. Privacy had always been a big element of her personality, and she believed, accordingly, that any problems she was having in her relationship were none of the public's business.

Unfortunately, all of her efforts as an actress would ultimately come to naught. *A Year in the Life* continued to be a critics' favorite, but, in an arena in which the bottom line is ratings, the show was lagging behind the pack. And so, as it neared the end of its first season, its future was in grave doubt. There was talk of giving it a partial renewal of six episodes to see if viewership would pick up. There was also an idea of rerunning the first season during the summer on a less competitive night to see if the ratings would improve. In the end, good reviews and all, *A Year in the Life* was canceled after the initial 22 episodes that aired between August 27, 1987, and April 20, 1988, on NBC. To say that Sarah was disappointed would be an understatement. In a short period of time, Sarah had delved deeply into her character and was mentally cataloging elements that she was looking forward to exploring in future shows. At the same time, she was grateful for the opportunities that the series had provided for her to progress as an actress. But in the wake of *A Year in the Life*, Sarah's stock would continue to rise in Hollywood, and the young actress would not be out of work for very long.

Over the next two years, she became a staple in television movies of the week, appearing in 1988's *Dadah Is Death*, about an Australian woman who attempts to save her son from the gallows. The movie, which starred Julie Christie, with a primarily Australian cast and crew, was filmed in Macao, then a Portuguese colony, now part of China. This was Sarah's first experience in working in another country. In 1989, she appeared in *Twist of Fate*, a standard-issue mystery, and the tear-jerkering bio film *The Ryan White Story*, about an AIDS-infected youngster whose mother attempts to have her dying son attend public school.

While she enjoyed being in demand, there was some concern that Sarah was once again being typecast, this time as a television actor. She was far from being a snob when it came to TV, fully aware that the small screen was capable of producing good work. But she was also aware that television actors traditionally had a hard time crossing over into movies and that the longer she stayed in television work the harder it would be to break into film. Consequently, Sarah began to become more picky when it came to choosing roles. Where much of her early work had been to establish a reputation and pay the bills without too much concern for quality, Sarah was now making a good story and a challenging character the criteria for future work. This attitude would occasionally put her in conflict with her agents, who, while agreeing that she should do only the best possible projects, thought that she should sometimes do less than sterling assignments, just for the sake of working. But her representatives could not argue with the degree of integrity their client insisted on having.

In the midst of her run as a television actress, her thoughts were never far from the New York stage. Sarah missed the edginess and spontaneity of stepping on the stage. And so, when some time opened up in what had become a nonstop work schedule in film and television in 1989, she returned to the Big Apple to appear in the Broadway production of Wendy Wasserstein's Pulitzer Prize-winning play *The Heidi Chronicles*. For Sarah, *The Heidi Chronicles* proved to be a constant challenge to her ego. Although she was no stranger to the stage, her acting skills had come to be very much influenced by her movie and television work. That she would be playing multiple characters was also a tall order. And so her cast members, who were older, more experienced, and more theater-oriented, often looked upon Sarah's very slow and methodical approach to her roles and the play with frustration.

Director Daniel Sullivan was very much in tune with what Sarah was trying to accomplish at the time and how it was putting her in direct conflict with the rest of the production. "I remember when I directed her in *The Heidi Chronicles*," he recalled in a *Los Angeles Times* interview. "Some of the other actors were frustrated because she put it [her character] together so organically. They wanted to do it [the pacing] faster. She always took the disdain of her elders in stride when they didn't feel she had the stage chops they had." And while they never really came around to her way of performing, in the end the rest of the cast had to admit that the finished product was quite in keeping with the tone and the emotional balance of the show. Credit Sarah with staying in control under circumstances that, creatively, were less than perfect and for showing a lot of poise in a potentially volatile situation.

For Sarah, half the fun of doing *The Heidi Chronicles* was being back in New York and renewing acquaintances with her circle of theater friends. During this visit, she also spent time with her parents and was happy to see that, with the older children moving out, things were not quite so hectic in that household. These visits also renewed the strong bond between Sarah and Barbara and allowed Sarah to assure her mother that, although things were not always the best with Downey, no matter what happened she would come out on top.

Following the successful, critically acclaimed run of *The Heidi Chronicles* as well as equally strong acting turns in the plays *Life under Water*, *Wrestlers* (directed by Burt Reynolds), and *April Snow*, Sarah's confidence knew no bounds. Sarah had proven herself to be an all-purpose actress who was equally comfortable on a stage or on the set of a movie or television show. This latest round of theater work had also succeeded in establishing her credentials as a multipurpose actor, someone who could play the lead as well as fully realized supporting characters. *A Year in the Life* had also finally succeeded in opening the eyes of producers to the idea that her unorthodox looks need not be a deterrent to certain sexy roles. But despite the more glamorous turn in *A Year in the Life*, she continued to play slightly off-kilter characters. And so, despite the fact that she was working nonstop, Sarah had real concerns that she had, by age 25, established herself as a type and thus limited herself at the same time. "For a while, I was on one track," she told the *Chicago Tribune*.

She returned to Hollywood, confident that the best was yet to come. And, once again, it was television that would allow her to open the door yet another crack. Lawyer shows had always been a television mainstay, guaranteed to gather an audience with dramatic cases and strong characters. Which is why *Equal Justice*, an hour-long series on ABC that focused on the Pittsburgh-district attorney's office, seemed to be a natural. On this show was a character that seemed to be ideal for Sarah. In fact, young attorney Jo Ann Harris, who was suddenly and reluctantly thrust into the arena of big-city prosecuting, shared a lot of the strengths and insecurities that Sarah herself possessed. Sarah was excited at the chance to play such a mature character. But she confessed in an *US* interview that she was reluctant to step back into the television series grind. "I was reticent to take the part because every TV show I do gets great ratings, [gets nominated for] Emmys, and is canceled. I was afraid of having it taken away again." But none of the current film offers looked promising for anything more than a paycheck, and Sarah did like the idea of dressing up in conservative business suits and taking on the bad guy. So eventually she gave in to the possibilities offered by *Equal Justice* and was rewarded with a well-rounded role in which, as the stories unfolded, she could play tough in the courtroom and be all too human outside it. Although the early ratings were only so-so, the reviews, not too surprisingly, were positive and noted that the promise Sarah had projected in *A Year in the Life* was fully realized in *Equal Justice*.

Sarah was convinced that *Equal Justice* was the reason that she was now being seriously considered for adult roles that she would not have had a chance at landing three years earlier. "I've been very lucky," she enthused in an *US* interview. "It's important to be perceived as someone who can change." Television continued to be good to Sarah. Not so quick to fall back on clichés, *Equal Justice* allowed her the opportunity to play a substantial, fully realized adult in a realistic setting. She was playing the tough real-life attorney and flip-flopping into emotion and sensitivity with ease. This was truly a solid portrayal by Sarah, who appeared to be coming of age with a series of defining, small-screen performances.

She was confident enough that when *Equal Justice* went on hiatus midway through 1990—the show ran on ABC from March 27, 1990, to January 9, 1991—she went looking for a solid film role to occupy her time and to salve her feelings about her deteriorating relationship with Downey. She found one in the modern-day urban fable called *L.A. Story*. Written by and starring Steve Martin, who had risen to comic prominence as a regular host on *Saturday Night Live* and in such films as *The Jerk* (1979), *All of Me* (1984), and *Planes, Trains, and Automobiles* (1989), *L.A. Story* tells the comic-tragic story of a burned-out television weatherman who learns how to handle life and love in a fantasy-filled midlife crisis in Los Angeles. Integral to the evolution of Martin's character is a

life-affirming relationship with a sexy, free-spirited Valley Girl
named SanDeE. In the past, it was a role totally out of the realm
of possibility for Sarah.

When Sarah first read the script for L.A. *Story*, with her growing confidence she thought she had a shot, but she had no idea
that Martin was involved. After she read the script and aced the
audition, she was astonished to find out who her costar would be.
She was both excited and nervous at the prospect of working with
Martin. A week later the phone rang, and the producers told her
they really wanted her for the role. Sarah was excited and then
apprehensive at the prospect of playing somebody who operated
in a totally odd, totally sexual way. She had never played such an
uninhibited role in her life. And she was scared. "When I found
out they had cast me as SanDeE, I thought they had made a
horrible mistake and that sooner or later, they would realize it,"
she told *Buzz*. "I was thrilled that I had gotten the part, but I was
also thinking, 'Shit, now I have to do this, and I have no idea who
she is.'"

In preparation for the role, Sarah began an intensive period of
study. Since SanDeE was, according to the story, a regular on the
Venice Beach scene, Sarah began hanging out at that beach in
the hope of running into her character in the flesh. But she soon
realized that SanDeE lived only on the pages of the script. She
rented every Steve Martin movie she could to get an idea of how
female characters had related to Martin's in previous films. She
sensed that actresses in his films had always been allowed their
comedic moments but ultimately played second fiddle to Martin
and his needs, so she was prepared to bring that element of support to the film. And then there was the matter of sex. L.A. *Story*
called for Sarah to be romantically and sexually involved with
Martin. She was horrified that the first day of filming would require
her to do a love scene with Martin. For a week prior to the start of
filming, she barely ate and spent all her time viewing every movie
she could think of that contained sex scenes to give her a better
idea of how she should act in bed and of the choreography of
movie sex. Her choice of films was decidedly odd. She looked to

Last Exit to Brooklyn, Miami Blues, Wild Orchid, and *Happy Together* for inspiration. But as she would later recall, nothing helped.

Consequently, Sarah was a bundle of nerves her first few days on the set of *L.A. Story.* "I thought they'd fire me because my hands were shaking," she told *Premiere* magazine. But Sarah survived the first days of filming and, in particular, the tastefully handled sex scene, at which she proved to be quite adept. What she also discovered as filming progressed was that Martin, despite rumors to the contrary, was a generous actor who encouraged her to exploit the character of SanDeE to full effect. With Martin's support, director Mick Jackson was constantly on a megaphone, encouraging her to be more animated but relaxed: "More bounce, Sarah." Martin "just stood there and let me be extremely large in the movie," she told the *New York Times.* "I went way over the top and he could have stopped it with a word." SanDeE was a cathartic moment for Sarah. The freewheeling character allowed her to explore emotions that she had not felt confident enough to access before. *L.A. Story* finally allowed her to fully blossom as an actor.

Sarah returned to *Equal Justice,* but the small-screen curse continued to follow her, and the show was canceled shortly after the completion of its first season in 1991. However, her disappointment was replaced with joy later that year when *L.A. Story* opened to rave reviews and powerful box office returns. The reviewers were quick to praise Sarah for what they believed would be a breakout role for the young actress. The *Hollywood Reporter's* review read "Keys to the city go to Sarah Jessica Parker for her frisky verve." The *Los Angeles Village View* offered the opinion that "Parker's flippant portrayal of a girl beyond space cadet range is right on the money." *Variety* proclaimed Parker a "scene stealer." The *Long Beach Press Telegram* stated that "Parker is a delightful free spirit." Sarah, to say the least, was thrilled with this sudden turnaround in the public's perception of her. "There was great satisfaction in people saying, 'Did you see her?'" she told *GQ.* "Because two weeks prior to being cast in *L.A. Story,* I wasn't sexy enough for the part. Now my agents don't have to say 'No, really, if you put enough makeup on her and a short skirt, she can look okay.'"

A star-making role, SanDeE allowed Sarah to access the little girl in her and channel it into a thoughtful, soulful, and believable portrait of a woman-child without a care. This was a tougher role than it appeared to be. Sarah managed to convey the fantasy and the vulnerability of this modern-day nymph and created the perfect counter to Martin's character's confusion without resorting to veiled cynicism. Sarah was overjoyed and placed the credit directly at the feet of Steve Martin. "I wanted to write him a note but I thought that would be kind of dorky," she recalled in a *New York Times* interview. "And you can't call a guy like that up and say 'Thanks for making me a star.'"

Finding Her Prince

5

Sarah's success would be bittersweet, for while she was basking in the glow of rave reviews for her work, she was saddened by the ending of her seven-year relationship with Downey. There were the tears, the guilt, but finally the resolution that she had to get on with her life. Even though her film career was on the rise in the rush of fame following the release of *L.A. Story*, Sarah was tempering the excitement with a bit of caution, an attribute that had become ingrained in her psyche due, in no small part, to the up-and-down nature of her chosen career. To be sure, she was now receiving a lot of scripts that she would not have been considered for in the past. In fact, they were arriving on her doorstep almost daily. But quantity does not mean quality, and Sarah was passing on more and more offers. Some offered cookie-cutter takes on her *L.A. Story* character wrapped around insubstantial story lines. Others were lightweight romps that would have required a degree of nudity or sexuality that Sarah was not comfortable with. Still others were just plain bad from top to bottom.

It was during this period in her life that Sarah took her mother's activist teachings to heart and began getting involved in various political and social causes. Her coming out as an activist was a gradual process, a by-product of her studious reading habits and seeming addiction to CNN. Sarah began to see the world as a less-than-perfect place for great segments of society and chose to try to do her part to make things better. Her choices were not always the expected celebrity-involved movements. She became involved in the American Civil Liberties Union and Planned Parenthood, and, as a member of the Hollywood Women's Political Committee, she became active in encouraging women to get involved in political causes. In later years, she became a leading fundraiser for UNICEF. Her thinking about being involving in such less-publicized causes was simple: there were people out there who needed help, and, if she was in a position to give it, she was going to.

Sarah had always insisted on maintaining close ties with the theater, no matter what shape her film career was in, so in 1991, with no film jobs on the horizon, she reunited with her *The Heidi Chronicles* director, Daniel Sullivan, for a six-month run in the taut drama *The Substance of Fire*. Five years later, the pair were reunited when they made the play into a film. Sarah's role, Sarah Geldhart, the daughter of a refugee from the Holocaust, turned out to be a powerful acting choice, one that was in marked contrast to her comedic breakout in *L.A. Story*. And although Sarah has always prided herself on being a diligent, dedicated, and extremely focused worker, this tale of a tragedy that ultimately rips a family apart offered a particularly challenging role due, in large part, to the fact that the play, written by Jon Robin Baitz, was very carefully constructed and allowed for little personal interpretation. "You have to pay attention to the words," she recalled in a *Los Angeles Times* interview. "I hate using stupid actor words, but there's a subtext you have to pay attention to. I usually prefer to be more instinctual."

Sarah was very happy with her part because she thought that there was substance in her character. It gave her the opportunity to play an extremely dramatic part after so many comedic roles. Sarah was ready to make the necessary adjustments. And the results? Looking back on the play, director Sullivan offered that "She is totally spontaneous and prepared. She's immediately there." Sarah will be the first to admit that *The Substance of Fire* was a struggle for her. She had made periodic forays into theater throughout her career, but coming off *L.A. Story* and other comedies Sarah was afraid that her dramatic chops were lacking. And that could be tough in a play that required the full palette of emotions. But that she would finally turn in a solid dramatic performance, rather than ride her current popularity into another comedy, was a sure indication that Sarah was a daring performer, willing to take certain risks for her personal and professional advancement.

Critical praise and good word of mouth quickly resulted in *The Substance of Fire* becoming one of the hottest tickets on Broadway, and the audience was regularly sprinkled with celebrities. One night John F. Kennedy Jr. was in the audience. The son of the late beloved president of the United States, he was easily one of the most eligible young bachelors at the time. A few years earlier, *People* magazine christened him "The Sexiest Man Alive." According to the tabloid reports, he had shown a propensity for dating young actresses, perhaps because he was a frustrated actor himself. Kennedy was instantly attracted to Sarah. After the performance, he went backstage. Sarah was impressed with his bearing and manners. "He's very nice," she told *Redbook* in July 1996. "He's very kind, clearly raised well." After exchanging pleasantries, Kennedy left, and Sarah assumed that would be the end of it since he had not asked her out or for her phone number. And it was not her style to ask a man out, despite her previous boldness with Robert Downey Jr. A couple of days later, Kennedy and Sarah ran into each other at the wedding of a mutual friend. The pair took advantage of the coincidence and continued the easygoing, getting-to-know-each-other process. But this time, Kennedy went away with Sarah's address. A few days later, Sarah received what she described as "a formal, lovely note" from Kennedy asking if she would join him for a meal. Sarah was not normally starstruck, but the idea that John F. Kennedy Jr. had asked her out on a date succeeded in shattering her veneer of composure. Sarah's close friend, choreographer Adam Shankman, recalled in *People*, "I remember when John Kennedy Jr. asked her out on a date. She called me, screaming, 'You're not going to believe who asked me out!'"

During their first few dates, Sarah's early impressions of Kennedy were confirmed. In a lighthearted mood, she told the *Advocate*, "I found him to be far more interesting as a conversationalist and much brighter than I had expected." Their relationship soon turned romantic, and, while Sarah has always remained quiet on the particulars, she did drop some hints to the *Advocate* about his body, his chest hair, and the cloverleaf tattoo Kennedy got shortly after they began dating. Sarah was beginning to feel more comfortable in their relationship, not that she was entertaining any thoughts that it might turn permanent. It was still too early for that. But the simple notion of being out and about on the arm of a handsome man of some substance and fame definitely had its appeal. It also eased the nagging insecurity that she was not pretty enough to attract the attention of someone like Kennedy. Going to the finest restaurants, attending the chicest gallery openings, and getting the best seats at the theater also figured into the fantasy element of the relationship for Sarah. If this were her own Cinderella story, she hoped the clock would never strike midnight.

Despite having gone through some of the tabloid histrionics while living with Robert Downey Jr., Sarah remained relatively naïve about the potential consequences of celebrity dating and, in particular, dating a Kennedy. She would quickly find out that, where Kennedys go, the spotlight is sure to follow. What Sarah would discover in dating a high-profile personality is that she never came off looking well. That was not a concern in their first few dates. Sarah was immediately captivated by Kennedy's down-to-earth demeanor and wide-ranging interests. Her sense of the man was that all the tragedies that had befallen him and his family had turned him soulful and introspective. Kennedy was completely different from Downey, and she liked that difference. No subjects were ever declared taboo between them, but certain things simply did not seem to come up often, perhaps due to a sense of respect for the other's privacy. Sarah could not recall if Kennedy ever questioned her about previous relationships and, in particular, Robert Downey Jr. She did recall that the topic of Kennedy's late father was only mentioned once and that she found Kennedy reflective and just a bit solitary when discussing the assassinated president of the United States. Sarah took his reaction as a sign not to bring it up again.

Although they dated only a few months, Sarah immediately found herself the subject of gossip columns and tabloid reports, and, although she had been what she once described as a "semi-public person" since her days in *Annie*, she would later admit that she had no idea what the consequence of real fame was until she began seeing Kennedy. "We would go places where there wasn't a soul around and the next day, I'd see pictures of us there in the tabloids," she remembered in a *New York Times* story. "He's a nice man, but for God's sake, I feel like I should apologize for dating him." Adding to her woes was the fact that the gossip columns were becoming increasingly nasty in their descriptions of their relationship. "It was very upsetting to me that, in the presses' view, I had become the ugly duckling who got lucky," she angrily recalled to the *Advocate*.

Kennedy had dealt with this level of press intrusion all his life and simply ignored it. He also assured Sarah that eventually they would get tired of stalking them and move on to somebody else. However, Sarah grew increasingly uncomfortable with the paparazzi shadowing their every move. The press intrusion became so bad that Sarah took to calling the tabloids and telling them that she had never been to the restaurant they had supposedly caught her at and that she would not do the things in public that their reporters had supposedly caught her doing with Kennedy. But the tabloid press would not let up. The lack of privacy reached critical mass when, after spending a weekend at a semiprivate seaside resort, the couple found themselves plastered all over every scandal sheet in New York.

Whether there was ever anything more than just a good friendship involved was open to conjecture, but eventually Sarah and Kennedy went their separate ways. In the aftermath of her relationship with Kennedy, Sarah was reflective and philosophical. She lamented the fact that they had never really gotten to know each other well enough to make the relationship emotionally satisfying for her and that the press stalking them was a contributing factor in their breakup. "After all is said and done, that's what I'll be remembered for," she sarcastically told *W Magazine* at that time. "It has become the defining factor in the person I am. It's pathetic. When I die, they're going to say 'Oh yeah, Sarah once dated John Kennedy.'" The final irony came when, shortly after breaking up with Sarah, Kennedy proclaimed that he would never date another actress. Within a matter of weeks, he was actively involved with Darryl Hannah.

There were the inevitable inquiries from the press about what had gone wrong, and when Sarah refused to divulge anything, journalists went ahead and printed their own speculations, which she studiously ignored. With family and friends, it was a lot tougher. Members of her close circle had been getting a vicarious thrill out of following Sarah and Kennedy's relationship, and while they were sympathetic they were also dying to know details. Sarah was polite but ultimately divulged little.

With Kennedy out of the picture, Sarah returned to a life of relative freedom. She would rarely date, preferring to hang out informally with friends or just be alone. Those who thought that Sarah was doing her best to cover a broken heart were off base. She had moved on with her life and was just enjoying New York and the moment. With no steady boyfriend, Sarah eventually turned her attentions to her fantasy man, David Letterman. The late-night television talk-show host with the big cigars and a fondness for deadpan humor was Sarah's true love and had been since 1979, when, as a preteen in Cincinnati, she would tune in daily to watch the largely unknown Letterman do his early morning regional show. Over the years, Sarah would watch him religiously on his late-night show and, as her star rose in the Hollywood universe, would occasionally appear on his show. They would usually end up shamelessly flirting with each other, and Letterman could be counted on to end up totally tongue-tied in her presence. "I've been watching this man since before there was any question of his heart being anything less than perfect," she enthused to the *New*

York Daily News. "He is so my type. He loves cigars and baseball. Isn't he the perfect red-blooded American male?" Over the years, Sarah has tactfully admitted that she would have loved to have gone out with him in her single days. But it was just not meant to be.

Her fears that she would be branded "the Kennedy woman" and that the quality of acting roles would decline proved to be unfounded as Sarah continued to find herself in demand on both the big and the small screens. Eventually, she decided to appear in another movie for television entitled *In the Best Interest of the Children*, yet another fact-based story of a young mother with mental problems who is faced with having to give up her five children to the foster care system. Sarah liked the idea of playing the mother, a role she was convinced would continue to showcase her dramatic skills and forever remove her from the stigma of teen roles.

Unhappily, *In the Best Interest of the Children* was the worst professional experience she had. The movie was shot in a cockroach-infested and trash-filled house in Iowa in the middle of summer. The child actors were inexperienced and undisciplined. Sarah, ever the perfectionist, did not think she was giving a good performance. And then there was the script. "The script was everything I didn't want it to be," she sadly reflected in *Buzz*. "I thought it was manipulative and just so obviously Movie of the Weekish. Nobody wanted to be offensive to anybody. I felt helpless." Quite simply, Sarah could only be as good as the script. And the script was a cliché-ridden mess. So could Sarah play cliché? She was surprised when television critics seemed to see through the film's mediocrity to find what they considered a solid and particularly effective performance in her portrayal of the tormented mother. Typical of the plaudits was the *People*: "Parker delivers a moving performance."

Fortunately, Hollywood has a short memory, and, despite concerns that appearing in *In the Best Interest of the Children* had set her back a step, it was not long before Sarah once again had several tempting offers. What caught her eye was a broad romantic comedy about a compulsive gambler who loses his fiancée to a mobster in a rigged card game. The film, with its plot twists and largely physical humor, once again played to Sarah's growing talents as a comedian. The fantasy-fairy-tale quality of *Honeymoon in Vegas* was enhanced by the glitz and glamor of the Las Vegas strip locations, and Sarah, feeling very much the little girl, was having the time of her life. Not that it was all easy. She was sharing the screen with Oscar-winning megastars James Caan, whose credits include *The Godfather* films, and Nicolas Cage. Her adrenaline was pumping throughout filming, and she is the first to admit that she suffered a severe case of nerves. She was able to control it—until the very last day of filming and the very last scene. "Take after take, I just couldn't do it," she confessed to *Premiere* magazine. "And the more I did it, the worse I got. My hands were shaking, my neck started itching, and I got a weird twitch. And everyone was gathered around the monitor watching this heinous act take place." It took a lot of takes, but she eventually got it right.

Honeymoon in Vegas writer-director Andrew Bergman didn't notice her nervousness. In fact, he praised her normalcy as the overriding factor in bringing believability to her sweet and naïve character, Betsy Nolan. "The reason she works so well in this movie is that there is nothing actressy about her. That's her strength as a person and also her strength on the screen."

Despite her nerves, Sarah enjoyed the work, and when she wasn't in a scene she just relaxed and enjoyed herself. She laughed out loud at the Flying Elvises scene and at Peter Boyle as Chief Orman.

Sarah always worked best when she was allowed to be herself, and she found the perfect fictional counterpart to her true nature in *Honeymoon in Vegas*. Given her personality, the sweet part was a cinch. But the conviction she exhibited in portraying first naïveté, then determination, and finally calm individuality was a bonus to the viewer and a sign that Sarah was an actor with depth. Reviewers instantly took notice of her maturing skills. The *Los Angeles Times* responded by saying, "Sarah Jessica Parker not only looks appropriately attractive but also brings an essential down to

STEVE SANDS / CORBIS OUTLINE

Sarah stars with Nicolas Cage in *Honeymoon in Vegas*

earth sanity to the role." The *New York Times* agreed: "Miss Parker is super as a young woman who behaves sanely without losing her great, good humor." The *Los Angeles Village View* exclaimed, "Parker's sweetness colors her in black and white simplicity." *Los Angeles Magazine* recognized that "Parker has become a sex symbol but in a vibrant and sexy way."

The fantasy relationship between Sarah and her costar Nicolas Cage was intense, so much so that, by the time filming completed on *Honeymoon in Vegas*, the couple were romantically involved. Cage, despite his wildly aggressive screen persona in such films as *Peggy Sue Got Married*, *Raising Arizona*, and *Moonstruck*, had a fairly easygoing and humane personality. It was widely known by this time that Cage was actually Francis Ford Coppola's nephew, but he had changed his name to establish an independent career. As with the early stages of her relationship with Robert Downey Jr., Sarah's intuitiveness immediately saw through the hype and the misconceptions and found the truly decent human being. Sarah would often acknowledge that while they were romantically linked she found the friendship with Cage an equal attraction. For Sarah, falling in love with her costar did not seem too outrageous, and, while there was heat in the relationship, she took an easy attitude toward Cage—at least in the beginning.

Once again, Sarah was quiet on the particulars of why the relationship began to slide. Which left it wide open to speculation. One rumor making the rounds was that Sarah, as with Downey during the last days of their relationship, was jealous that her partner's career had, to that point, eclipsed hers. Another unsubstantiated report was that Cage was too much of a party guy to mesh with her basic stay-at-home style. Still another claimed that Cage was, in fact, cheating on her. Since Sarah and Cage were not talking about their relationship, those rumors were quickly confined to the realm of tabloid fantasy. The fact that Sarah would often look back on her nearly year-long relationship with Cage in the most complimentary terms, often referring to him as "a wonderful traveling companion and a great friend," would seem to nullify most of the tabloid scenarios. In later years, Sarah, without going into great detail, conceded that their breakup was messy. "I'd be perfectly happy to stay in touch," she once told W Magazine in looking back on her relationship with Cage. "But it's not allowed. People don't feel comfortable."

On the surface, Sarah was fine with the fact that things had not worked out with Cage, but below the surface there was some turmoil. At age 26, Sarah was suddenly obsessed with the idea of settling down and having children. And, at the very moment when her career was beginning to take off, she would privately and just as often publicly make it plain that she would willingly walk away from acting for the domestic life of wife and mother. "I can't wait to have a husband and children," Sarah told the St. Louis Post-Dispatch not long after her split with Cage. "To be held accountable and be responsible and have a child throw up on my shoulder and have to get kids off to school and be completely harried and try to have a life. I can't wait to be tired and exhausted and cranky and love my husband and hate him. I can't wait." She went on to admit that her idea of domestic bliss was pretty much a dream at that point since her career was taking precedence over a social life.

Sarah had never been one to date a lot. She saw her romantic life as a matter of chance, and she did not foresee her approach to love changing in the immediate future. However, chance did not always make for happy times, as she explained in an *IC Showbiz. com* interview. "I am certainly familiar with the pain of being single and searching for something in the dating scene. It's a role I'd become painfully accustomed to in my life."

As was her pattern, Sarah had taken some time off following the completion of *Honeymoon in Vegas*, and, as her relationship with Cage began to disintegrate, she began spending more time in and around her home in New York. It was a time of simple pleasures—sleeping late, taking leisurely walks, having breakfasts in and around Greenwich Village, and catching up on what her family was doing. As always, she did not date actively. "I didn't really make a habit of dating because it was so scary, ridiculously difficult, and intimidating," she candidly said in the *Toronto Sun*. "If I stumbled upon someone or they stumbled upon me, and they weren't evil as far as I could tell, and they asked me out for dinner, then I went out on a date. But I didn't search to meet somebody. That's not in my nature."

What was high on her agenda at the time was to be supportive of the acting efforts of her brothers and sisters. And so one night she ventured into the theater district, where her brothers Toby and Pippen were appearing in a play. Afterward, Toby introduced his sister to the play's director. Matthew Broderick was a veteran actor on both stage and screen, starring in such films as *Ferris Bueller's Day Off* (1986), *Biloxi Blues* (1988), and *The Freshman* (1990). While Sarah would later concede that it was not exactly love at first sight, there was something about him that was hard to resist. A few days later, she tagged along with Toby and Matthew on an informal night at the movies. It was a gradual process. To Sarah, Matthew seemed to be laid back and confident, and their values and politics seemed to mesh. Her initial reaction was that he was someone she would like to get to know better. And Matthew seemed to be interested in her as well, but he was cautious. He had been involved in several long-term, albeit low-profile, relationships over the years, the most notable being with actresses Helen Hunt and Jennifer Grey. While not wounded by love, Matthew would later admit that he was a little skittish about even the hint of a relationship, but he liked Sarah, so eventually he would have to work up his courage.

After that night, Sarah often fantasized about Matthew asking her out. But as the days and weeks went by and there was no call, Sarah, still unwilling to call up a man for a date, assumed he was not interested in her. Three months after their first meeting, Matthew called her up and left a very charming and self-effacing message asking her out. Matthew left the decision about where to go up to Sarah, who suggested a comfortable West Village dive called The Bagel, but there was a change of plans, and the couple ended up at the more sedate Cornelia Street Café. Their first date was a decidedly low-key event—dinner and the theater. Sarah, normally calm and collected in dating situations and more than willing to let the man take the lead, was unexpectedly nervous in the face of what she would later describe as Matthew's "lethal charm," and throughout dinner she talked almost nonstop. Broderick stared at her and occasionally punctuated the largely one-sided conversation with a funny story or anecdote of his own. Long known in the Hollywood community as a stolid, serious person, the actor was showing Sarah a side few people had seen—the funny side, the sweet side. By the end of that first date, Sarah had been charmed, and despite the little voice that said "be cautious" she was hopelessly and completely in love. Matthew, who had been notoriously closed-mouthed when it came to expressing his feelings for women, was likewise taken in by Sarah's bubbly personality, enthusiasm, and wide-ranging interests and obvious intelligence. The couple became inseparable and, within a few months, had moved in together.

Sarah's family and friends were concerned that the couple had become too close too fast. For many, the memory of what Sarah had gone through living with Robert Downey Jr. was still fresh. But Sarah had no qualms. Matthew was not into drugs, drank only socially, and was not a big party guy. He was nothing like Downey. And because of his low-profile nature, she did not foresee the tabloid assault that had highlighted her time with Kennedy.

As their relationship grew, Sarah found new things about Matthew to respect and admire almost daily. Despite being a veteran of both Hollywood films and the Broadway stage, he was a very low-key person. He was also frugal. Coming from a poor background, Matthew would take the subway or ride his bike rather than take a taxi, which was a delight to Sarah. She loved his honesty, sincerity, and sense of humor. When they were out in public, she liked the way he interacted with people, coming across as somebody completely at ease with his surroundings. And Matthew and Sarah seemed to have the same interests. A night out at the theater, a late breakfast or dinner, running or rollerblading, or walking Matthew's dog, Sally, were grand public appearances. Occasionally, they would be seen together at a movie premiere or a Hollywood party, but they were basically homebodies who would squabble over things like who got what section of the *New York Times* first. They could usually be found at home, where Sarah would often indulge her penchant for cooking big and not always healthy meals. She had a fondness for bread, potatoes, and other high-calorie foods, but her fast metabolism meant that she quickly burned off whatever she ate.

In those early days together, Sarah and Matthew remained cautious. They agreed to share all expenses and to keep separate checking accounts. These coldly logical decisions appealed to Sarah and further cemented their relationship in her eyes.

Professionally, Matthew's career was more advanced than Sarah's, but even that turned out to be a plus in the relationship. Knowing the realities of the acting business, Matthew was not upset when Sarah had to leave for weeks on end for a film. With his experience, he was also quite handy in helping Sarah determine whether a particular job was worthwhile. "He's one of the smartest men I've ever known," she cooed in a *Redbook* interview.

Sarah with the love of her life, Matthew Broderic

"He's incredibly charming and he's the most handsome man I've ever laid my eyes on. And the best part of it all is that he loves me." Her fantasy had seemingly come through, and, at that point, she would have been content to lie back and just revel in the good feelings the relationship brought her.

However, finding true love coincided nicely with the latest round of offerings from Hollywood. Disney came calling with *Hocus Pocus*, a comedy centered on a lonely teen who conjures up three long-deceased witches who sustain themselves by sucking the life out of children. Sarah's impression was that the comedy was edgy stuff by Disney standards, and with Bette Midler already attached Sarah decided that it was a win-win situation. Coincidentally, the film's director, Kenny Ortega, had also directed Matthew's breakout film, *Ferris Bueller's Day Off* (1986).

But while *Hocus Pocus* turned out to be a fun filmmaking experience, in which Sarah was impressive in the more comic moments as the lusty member of the witch trio, something happened, as it often does, between the completion of filming and the finished film. Many of the scenes in which Sarah appeared at her comedic best were either completely edited out or trimmed to the point where Sarah came across as nothing more than a glorified extra. She chalked up her *Hocus Pocus* experience as just another one of those sad Hollywood stories. "I haven't experienced editing to this degree before," she lamented in *Entertainment Weekly*. "I understand the choices that they made. I just wish they had left in a lot of the weird moments." Sarah's work in *Hocus Pocus* remains a mystery. There are only occasional glimpses of her comedic talent in the truncated version that played in theaters. Since the movie bombed at the box office, we may never see a director's cut that would show the true strength of Sarah's performance. Consequently, what viewers are left with, in terms of Sarah's talent, is a slight, inconsequential performance that she would probably be better off deleting from her résumé. *Hocus Pocus* did not fare well with critics. Neither did Sarah. *Los Angeles Village View* quipped, "A few of the film's more risqué moments, namely Parker's cleavage, will be lost on the small fry." The *Hollywood Reporter* offhandedly said, "Parker with her spastically sexy movements holds her own."

Shooting *Hocus Pocus* in the middle of summer was also an ordeal for the actress. The tension surrounding the production and the heat resulted in Sarah losing a lot of weight and emerging from the process in need of a physical and emotional rest. A doctor prescribed total rest and relaxation, so a good part of the summer of '92 was spent doing absolutely nothing. While she was never in any real danger, the experience taught her a valuable lesson. Not to take her career all that seriously.

After her period of rest and relaxation, Sarah jumped into her first big-time Hollywood action film, *Striking Distance*, which starred the reigning action king, Bruce Willis, as a rogue Pittsburgh river cop whose unorthodox style of meting out justice puts him head to head with a serial killer. The impression around Hollywood was that *Striking Distance* was pretty unoriginal and uninspired and that all the principals were basically in it for the money. But it had been strongly suggested by her agents that it would give her career what they thought was a much-needed boost to be in a high-profile and blatantly commercial action film. The film immediately put her in a crisis of conscience. Her role as Willis's partner required her to handle a gun. "I vowed I would never do that," she recalled. But she was diligent about practicing holding the gun in a natural manner. Willis eventually offered to help her out. Although she felt competent at that point, she laughingly recalled how she conveniently forgot everything she had taught herself to stroke her costar's ego.

Striking Distance turned out to be an endless series of challenges. Learning to act on a boat as it raced up and down the river was a struggle that often ended up in a series of hilarious outtakes of pratfalls. There were many scenes in which Sarah had to run and jump on swaying decks very close to the water. Some scenes had to be shot 10 times or more. She also had to fight to keep a straight face in the fairly predictable, unartistic dialogue she had to utter. That she got along with Willis proved a plus since the film called for her to have a romantic liaison with the actor, which she handled with aplomb. But while *Striking Distance* was a lot of fun to make, Sarah was less than complimentary in her assessment of the film and thought it was a typical Hollywood epic— slick but ultimately empty. "I did this crapola with Bruce Willis called *Striking Distance*," she told *Redbook* in assessing her career. "That was an embarrassment." In later interviews, Sarah backtracked and tried to deny that she had dissed the film, and she worked the subject around to how shooting on water was difficult and how she had worked harder on *Striking Distance* than on any other film.

Along the way, Sarah discovered a lot about how studio interference and the politics of filmmaking can short-circuit even a derivative effort like *Striking Distance*. "From the first day on, the story changed," she reported to GQ. "I wasn't a participant in those changes, and that was frustrating. When you're number two on the call sheet, you expect to be a part of stuff. It [the movie] became more violent, which was upsetting because I abhor those films."

Even though Sarah had been working for a long time, *Striking Distance* was very much a dues-paying experience. She was given stock situations and not much to do within them. That the character was essentially a cipher, and a rather predictable one at that, did not make things any easier. Sarah has not done another straight-ahead action film since *Striking Distance*, which shows how distasteful the experience was and perhaps that she is not well suited to a conventional role. Reviewers panned the film and were quick to damn Sarah with faint praise. *People* described Parker's performance thus: "Parker is likeable, though seemingly the most adolescent, unjaded cop of all time." *Entertainment Weekly* seconded that notion when it proclaimed, "Sarah Jessica Parker is the only one in the movie who doesn't look sleep deprived."

Sarah was admittedly in a transitional phase of both her personal and her professional lives by 1993. She was stretching as an actress, had found a strong new love with Matthew Broderick, and was looking to the future with a positive state of mind. But she was also realistic, especially on the professional front. "I'm one of those people who has not had a meteoric rise," she stated in *Entertainment Weekly*. "So I don't expect anything to happen overnight."

Plan Nine from Tim Burton

6

Sarah had it all. Her career was moving along well, and she was in a position to choose projects rather than take whatever came along. And she had found her Prince Charming in Matthew Broderick. Everything was blue skies and red roses.

Given her state of bliss, Sarah decided to fill one of the voids from her past. She decided to try to reestablish contact with her biological father. Stephen Parker had always remained on the periphery of her life. He would occasionally check in, usually with Barbara, to see how the children were doing, but he had never offered much emotional support. Sarah was admittedly conflicted as she tracked her father down and had the first tentative meetings with him. She insisted that renewing her relationship with Parker should not be perceived as a slight to her stepfather and that the attempt to find her father was simply another facet of her life that she wanted to pursue. "I was feeling like a textbook case of an abandoned child," she confessed to the *New York Times*. "And I didn't like it at all. Also, with your father, how can you hold a grudge forever?" From all indications, Sarah's meeting with her biological father was cordial, if a bit tentative, and went a long way toward smoothing out relations between them, although Parker would remain marginal in his daughter's life from that point on.

Her father had always told her she was beautiful, but Sarah herself was not as sure. Although the question of her looks would occasionally surface to batter her ego, Sarah thought that since *L.A. Story* Hollywood had finally figured out that it was her talent and not necessarily her looks that was important. But her insecurities about her looks once again came into question in 1993 when she auditioned for the lead in the romantic comedy *Four Weddings and a Funeral.* The film, built on a wry sense of humor and happenstance between the two leads, was similar in some ways to *L.A. Story.* But Sarah immediately saw the female lead as a decided step up in terms of sophistication. It was a role that would cast her in a whole new light. The audition was highly competitive and included some of the biggest names in the business, but Sarah found herself on the short list of actresses up for the coveted part. In the end, the role was given to Andie MacDowell. Although Sarah would occasionally lose out to other actresses, missing out on *Four Weddings and a Funeral* was a particular disappointment. Sarah tried to put a philosophical face on her disappointment, but in a candid interview with *Movie-TV News* she admitted that she thought that losing the role was once again a not-too-subtle knock against her looks. "I'm not particularly proud of how I look," she said. "I've never been what Hollywood considers beautiful. It would be so great to look like Andie MacDowell. She beat me for the part in *Four Weddings and a Funeral.* She's so beautiful. I'd have hired her, too."

During the audition process for *Four Weddings and a Funeral,* Sarah and Matthew met the film's star, Hugh Grant, and his girl-friend, actress Elizabeth Hurley. It was a revelation for Sarah and Matthew. They went out to dinner several times while the couple were in New York, and, while they seemed to get along well, Sarah would later recall that they were bowled over by Grant and Hurley's British sophistication and felt a little awkward around them. Although they realized that they would never become close friends, they did continue to see the other couple.

Sarah's relationship with Matthew continued to be a light in her life—so much so that by 1994 Sarah was once again being very public in her desire to get married and have children. In

Sarah and Chris Noth shooting a scene from "Sex and the City"

The women of "Sex and the City" from left: Kim Cattrall, Kristin Davis, Sarah Jessica Parker, Cynthia Nixon

Celebrating her 2001 Golden Globe win

Sarah Jessica Parker and Chris Noth joke around
on the set of "Sex and the City"

fact, during an appearance on *The David Letterman Show*, the personable host and longtime hero of Sarah's innocently asked his guest "How's Matthew?" Sarah blurted out to a national television audience, "He's fine. He'd be perfect if he'd just marry me." As soon as she said it, Sarah knew she had made a big mistake. One of the things that Sarah loved about Matthew was that he was a very private person. He felt very strongly that certain things were fodder for the public and was more than willing to regale an audience with stories. But he had long been dead set against the topic of marriage as talk-show material. He reasoned, quite logically, that it was nobody's business. Needless to say, when Sarah got home from the *Letterman Show*, she caught holy hell from Broderick—quietly, of course.

It was one of only a handful of times that Sarah felt guilty after a confrontation with Matthew. And although things seemed to patch themselves up rather quickly, there remained a degree of guilt on Sarah's part for violating a pact they had agreed to regarding their privacy. From the beginning, Sarah and Matthew had been up-front with each other on the topic of marriage and children. Sarah wanted both very much. Matthew was extremely reluctant, and by 1994 Sarah, the occasional slip aside, had decided that the subject should be taboo.

But it remained a source of frustration for Sarah and the closest thing to a problem in their relationship. For a long time following the *Letterman* appearance, the marriage question became an integral part of any interview with either of the actors. Their responses would often be couched in humorous or flip tones, but reporters tended to jump to their own conclusions. Consequently, Matthew would often come across as the all-too-reluctant suitor and Sarah as the almost stereotypical desperate woman. Neither picture was very flattering and only seemed to add to an underlying uneasiness about this one element in an otherwise perfect relationship. "He's well aware of the fact that I want to be married and have kids more than anything," she told W *Magazine* in a moment of extreme candor. "I don't know what he wants. He's very undecided. So I don't talk about it with him any more. I have no interest in nagging him and having him listen to my fantasies. He can come to his own decision."

Following the back-to-back box office flops of *Hocus Pocus* and *Striking Distance*, Sarah was less inclined to jump into another mainstream film and, perhaps owing to her adherence to the spartan ethics of the theater, was looking for a more unorthodox choice for her next film. She found the perfect choice in director Tim Burton's *Ed Wood*, the story of B-movie, cross-dressing film director Edward D. Wood Jr., who, single-handedly, was responsible for such awful pictures as *Plan 9 from Outer Space* and *Glen or Glenda?* Burton, on the strength of films like *Pee-wee's Big Adventure*, *Beetlejuice*, and *Batman*, had become the poster boy for the new wave of unorthodox filmmaking. And the often staid Hollywood film community was finding itself drawn to his boyish comic book instincts. The consensus was that *Ed Wood* would be anything but the typical Hollywood biopic, and, not surprisingly, it became a magnet for such equally offbeat actors as Johnny Depp and Bill Murray.

The trashy nature of low-budget filmmaking in the 1950s and the decidedly period nature of the film looked to Sarah like good fun and an acting stretch. But given the eccentric nature of Tim Burton, Sarah was not surprised when her audition for the film was equally unusual. For one thing, there was no formal audition. Burton simply invited the actress to his office, and they talked about the story for a while. He then gave her a copy of the script, some of Ed Wood's movies, and instructions to give him a call after she had read and watched everything.

Sarah was amused and, once she stopped laughing, amazed that this array of strange characters had actually existed and that films this excruciatingly bad had ever been made. She was also at a loss as to which character she would play. She sensed that she might make a good Vampira but did not have a clue as to what Burton had in mind. So she called him and asked. She was shocked when the director, in his typical clipped manner, said "Delores." The character of Delores Fuller was the female lead. As Ed Wood's girlfriend, she goes through many changes as she comes to grips with the fact that Wood is a transvestite, and it is one of the biggest, most pivotal roles in the film. Sarah was so fascinated by the complexity of the part that she willingly put on weight to match her character's physical appearance and altered her attitude to match her white-trash on-screen persona.

When filming began, Sarah also discovered that director Burton, whom she admittedly thought was an odd guy, was actually quite normal. "I thought Tim Burton would be weird and withdrawn and odd and hard to talk to," she told W *Magazine*. "But he was lovely and charming and shy, and he had a vision. He didn't need to talk to you endlessly." It was a filmmaking experience in which Sarah literally had a hard time keeping a straight face. One day, it would be a scene with Bill Murray, whose sexually ambiguous character, Bunny, pranced about in a French-tip manicure and pearls. On another, Johnny Depp, as Ed Wood, would sashay around the set in an Angora sweater or a gown.

Although Sarah was not involved in much of the film's core relationship between Ed Wood and his "star" Bela Lugosi, played by Martin Landau (for which he won an Oscar), she could appreciate the obvious love and respect that played out between those two larger-than-life characters amid the chaos that was their lives. Lugosi was a fixture of the horror films of the 1930s and 1940s after playing the seminal Dracula (1931), but by the time he had met up with Edward Wood his reputation was in ruins. And when it came to her scenes, Sarah was grateful that Burton was at the controls. She was somewhat tentative at first, fearing that Delores would be too over the top and become little more than camp and cheap impersonation. But with his subtle guidance and willingness to let her try different things, Sarah soon became comfortable in the role and confident that she was bringing an accurate picture of the actress to life. And with Burton's eye for detail, Sarah found it fascinating to witness the emphasis on getting every nuance in re-creating some classically bad filmmaking. The *Plan 9 from Outer Space* sequences were a particular hoot, as Burton guided them through shabby graveyard sets and bad flying saucer interiors with all the twisted insight that Wood himself must have shown. If there was such a thing as method directing, Sarah was seeing it in Burton. Her role as Delores was the embodiment of the dreadful B-movie actress. Landau as Lugosi was a triumph, and he justifiably won an Oscar for his performance, perfectly mirroring the horror actor's quirks and mannerisms. Johnny Depp created the perfect Ed Wood—soft yet determined in valiantly trying to overcome the obstacles of Hollywood in the 1950s.

Perhaps more than her breakout role in *L.A. Story*, *Ed Wood* introduced the world to a Sarah Jessica Parker capable of doing "the actor thing," gaining the necessary weight, doing the quasi-method thing in going against type, and finding that she could fit rather easily into an extremely wacky film. And it was reflected in the reviews that seemed to get the joke of the film. *People* remarked that, "Parker has an intriguing, oblique quality." The *Los Angeles Village View* opined, "Sarah Jessica Parker is delightfully campy." *Rolling Stone* stated that "Sarah Jessica Parker is a wicked send up of Fuller's stiff emoting." The *New Yorker* offered, "Sarah Jessica Parker is engaging." And, in a backhanded compliment, *Variety* exclaimed, "Parker niftily pulls off some deliberately bad acting."

By 1995, Sarah had continued to build on her reputation as a solid, quirky actress who could make believable any number of wildly divergent characters. She was not yet a star-level actress, but her insistence on being real and professional in front of the camera had put her very much in demand. Not that Sarah was always so anxious to rise to the next level. In fact, while she did crave the spotlight, she was steadfastly resisting the stereotyping that would almost certainly guarantee her celebrity status. "What makes a real movie star is when you give the audience exactly what they want," she explained to the *Los Angeles Times*. "And I will never achieve that because that's my biggest fear . . . being the same." This was the ongoing tug of war in Sarah's professional life. Even at this relatively late point in her career, Sarah was having a tough time compromising. More films like *Honeymoon in Vegas* and *L.A. Story* and fewer like *Ed Wood*, despite the growth it allowed her as an actress, might have given her a higher level of commercial stardom. But Sarah remained loath to give up on the eccentric elements of what she was doing. That she could jump back and forth was a notion that continued to stay with her.

Which is why, following *Ed Wood*, Sarah agreed to do the shamelessly mainstream television remake of *The Sunshine Boys*, which starred Woody Allen, Peter Falk, and Edie Falco, who went on to fame in the HBO hit series *The Sopranos*. Oddly, Falk, not Allen, played the neurotic. It was shot in New York City under the direction of TV veteran John Erman, whose credits included *The Flying Nun, Roots,* and *The Bob Newhart Show*. Admittedly a minor work in which Sarah played the token spunky relative, in it she once again proved adept at broad comedy, and, she would later admit, she would have been crazy to pass up an opportunity to work with Woody Allen.

But agreeing to do *The Sunshine Boys* might have been a tactical error. Although it was a joy to watch Woody Allen and Peter Falk work, Sarah sensed that the show was not working. Her gut feeling would prove correct. Unfortunately, *The Sunshine Boys* was a weak effort even by television standards, mired, as it was, in stock, predictable, and decidedly old-fashioned situations and, despite Allen's participation, not offering many laughs. Airing was delayed for over a year amid charges that the film was extremely weak and unfunny. Even Neil Simon, who wrote the original play, was hard pressed to say anything good about it. When *The Sunshine Boys* did air on CBS's *Hallmark Hall of Fame* on December 29, 1997, it was, indeed, not very funny, and Sarah received her share of the criticism. *Variety* said, "Parker doesn't lend much depth to the role of the niece." But there was occasional praise as when the *New York Times* said, "Sarah Jessica Parker is engaging."

At this point, Sarah was at a crossroads. As far as Hollywood was concerned, she was beginning to settle into a type—the high-spirited girlfriend/sexual conscience of a male lead—as the consequence of her breakout role in *L.A. Story*. And while, within that context, the parts and the pictures were getting better, Sarah did not want to settle into that niche and began looking once again to the theater for a challenge. After the lame TV comedy, Sarah won the female lead in a much more solid comedy, *Miami Rhapsody*. The script, centering on an ad executive who is so disillusioned by love that she sabotages her own engagement, was intriguing. To Sarah, the story asked some important questions about love and independence. And she liked the opportunity to play a good-naturedly devious and calculating woman. Alternately cynical and bittersweet, *Miami Rhapsody* was her first starring role in a film since *Girls Just Want to Have Fun*. The fact that Disney was backing the project also meant that the film would get wide distribution and increase her profile with mainstream audiences.

During the making of *Miami Rhapsody*, which also featured Mia Farrow and Antonio Banderas, Sarah discovered a talent she did not realize she had—the ability to play believable pathos within the context of sophisticated and intelligent comedy. Sarah was the model of professionalism during the shoot. She mixed easily with her costars and, when in character, made the most of this rarely exercised dimension of cynicism. Adding to the strong outing in this film was an amazing growth in the sexual tension she brought to the screen. She was a cunning and aware beauty whose sexual desires came across in broad brush strokes. "I had never played a role like that before," she enthused to the *Los Angeles Times*. "It was the type of role that was traditionally reserved for men." The film's director, David Frankel, was a veteran of TV comedy, and, having worked with the likes of Ellen DeGeneres, he knew something about comedy. He watched daily Sarah's emergence as a complete actress and proclaimed, after the filming, that Sarah was one of the leading comediennes of her generation.

The advance word of mouth was very good on *Miami Rhapsody*, and the early reviews were all nearly unanimous in their praise for Sarah. Unfortunately, the film's release ran afoul of the latest realignment of studio executives at Disney. A number of studio heads, including chairman Jeffrey Katzenberg, left Disney and were replaced by people who were intent on wiping the old regime's slate clean. Consequently, *Miami Rhapsody*, which had been slated for a major national release, had its release and marketing campaign drastically cut. The result was disappointing box office sales and a quick exit from theater screens.

To say the least, Parker was disappointed. She had been counting on *Miami Rhapsody* to give her more clout with the studios as well as broaden her fan base. But she could console herself with some of the best, and occasionally tongue-in-cheek, reviews she had ever received. *Entertainment Weekly's* rave cast a particularly bright spotlight on Parker. "Parker, who delivers her pithy lines with the self-absorbed timing of a sexy cardsharp, is essentially a brilliant one-woman show. Parker, at once vibrant and snarky, gives her first fully commanding screen performance." The *New Republic* applauded Sarah: "She handles her part like a classy surfer, easily riding the crests and dips." The *Los Angeles Magazine* reviewer joked that "Sarah Jessica Parker is Woody Allen but with better biceps." *People* joshed, "Parker has made a rapid journey from cute to cutesy." Sarah had effectively made the leap from cute and innocent to hip, worldly, and cynical, avoiding the stumbles and clichés of twentysomething angst and showing the filmmaking community that she could play mightily against type.

Sarah turned 30 shortly after the completion of *Miami Rhapsody*. Personally and professionally, she was in a very good place. She had the man of her dreams in a relationship that, to her circle of friends, seemed too good to be true. And she had a career that had evolved from typecast roles into wide-ranging opportunities.

Sarah had long ago proclaimed that she would never leave the theater and had always insisted that she would do at least one play a year, no matter what her circumstances. However, the whirl of film offers had kept her from doing any theater work since 1991. She once again craved the rush of a live performance. And, as far as she was concerned, the more offbeat the better. Which is why she had to stifle a laugh when she was offered the only nonhuman role in the play *Sylvia*. Written by A.R. Gurney, the play tells the story of the declining relationship of a middle-aged couple whose life, unknown to them, is being manipulated by their family dog, Sylvia, a strange combination of Labrador and poodle, a stray that had been found and brought home by the husband. The small cast included actors Charles Kimbrough and Blythe Danner as the troubled couple. The challenge that Sarah chose to accept was to play the part of the dog without a costume and in human form.

Sylvia was truly experimental and challenged her acting skills. There were no rules or reference points for playing a dog in human form because no one else had ever done it. But Sarah instantly became aware of some elements that helped her to craft the character. She could not be too much human or too much dog. Her Sylvia could not be cloying or cutesy. "In many respects, this is the most complex role of my career," she told the *New York Times* during rehearsals for the play. "I want this dog to be sassy and provocative and coquettish and manipulative and sweet and flawed and all those things."

The challenge was to find a comparable human-animal relationship to model her character after. Sarah soon realized that she had the ideal template for Sylvia in the relationship between Matthew and his dog, Sally. And so she began an unobtrusive but focused examination of the interaction between her lover and his pet. Such mundane things as the way Sally would approach Matthew, where and how she would lie down, and how Matthew would pet the dog became overriding interests to Sarah. During the rehearsal stage, she would snuggle, climb on furniture, throw herself on the ground, and kiss people. Sarah was trying hard for accuracy while trying not to come across as sentimental or gimmicky.

Director John Trillinger had a reputation for taking chances and pushing the envelope, yet he marveled at the levels of improvisation Sarah built into the admittedly difficult role. He saw her doing a variety of strange doglike behaviors while still trying to make the character believable.

Sarah was nervous opening night. She thought that she had a firm grip on her four-legged character, but she also knew that the biggest critics in town would be in the audience, and, this being Off Broadway, it would only take a couple of bad reviews to torpedo the show. "The night the critics came, all the big shots were there, and there wasn't a laugh in the house," she painfully recalled in the *Christian Science Monitor*. "After the show I was crying. We were afraid they wouldn't see the fun in it, the love in it." Although they didn't laugh, the reviewers loved the show. *Sylvia* opened to rave reviews in which Sarah was inevitably applauded for making Sylvia integral to the story's development rather than merely cute and cuddly.

But, for her, the true test of the performance was to have Matthew see the play. And so one night Broderick stopped by. "I was enthralled," he said. "It was an odd feeling. It was like seeing my dog on stage, because she reminded me so much of Sally. And then I came home and saw Sally and thought, 'Wow, she's acting just like Sarah.'"

Alternately whimsical and dramatic, this was Sarah's most risky midcareer work. Sarah plumbed the depths of her talents in attempting this highly experimental role. To her credit, she deftly avoided the inherent gimmickry and overt cuteness of the part and turned in a believable creation.

Reviewers ate up her portrayal, giving Sarah raves. The *New Leader* stated, "Parker woofs, snorts, barks, and growls with the lunatic vitality of a canine." *Backstage* offered, "Parker is superb, a formidable talent." The *Christian Science Monitor* praised, "The humor of the piece derives mainly from watching Parker."

The success of *Sylvia*, which ran for about six months playing before sellout crowds, resulted in a number of varied film and theater offers. Going into 1996, Sarah was all over the acting spectrum. In her theater work, she was taking enormous risks, and, as a film actress, she was proving her diversity in both mainstream and more intimate productions. It was a heady time for the actress and, in a sense, a time for decision making.

Sarah had always valued her time off, particularly since she had been with Matthew. Their years together were always marked by periods when they were both working and apart. And the fact that Broderick had, coincidentally, just entered a rather prolific period in his career and had a full slate of film and theater roles made it easier for Sarah to say yes to everything. Her willingness to never turn anything down continued to have a lot to do with her childhood insecurities and the classic actor's fear that it could all disappear at any time. Not that Sarah would publicly admit to it. "Frankly it's just hard for me to say no," she once confessed.

The first thing she said yes to was *The First Wives Club*, a high-concept, star-studded comedy that featured Bette Midler, Diane Keaton, Goldie Hawn, Maggie Smith, and Stockard Channing as wronged women who get even with their former spouses. For Sarah, the role was almost a cliché. The attractive, husband-stealing Shelly was another, albeit more substantial, variation on the role of SanDeE from *L.A. Story*. Producers seemed to be fixated on that role for her.

This was a scattershot performance for Sarah. With most of the good lines going to the film's stars, she was faced with the formidable task of having to win small victories in scenes with little direction other than to advance the story line and justify actions that would come later. Sarah alternated between being in awe of her high-profile costars and focusing on her role. She turned in a solid performance in what many saw as a thin character. But Sarah's trophy woman succeeded in being spirited in a largely thankless role. Because the film was loaded with stars, Sarah did get her fair share of critical notices. *Rolling Stone* raved that the caricature of "a leggy gold digger was expertly spoofed by Sarah Jessica Parker." *L.A. Weekly* said simply that she "shines brightly," while the *New York Times* proclaimed that she was "slyly good." *Variety* added to the good cheer when it called her performance "memorable."

That Sarah was instinctively comfortable in this kind of role was a given, but she also added different shadings and nuances that elevated the part well beyond mere cliché. Needless to say, the actress enjoyed playing alongside some of the industry's most talented women. She admitted to being initially shy around the trio of superstars, but she soon discovered that they were warm and inviting people as well. In the end, Sarah was quite happy to play support in a movie that would go on to be one of 1996's top films.

Her next film, *Extreme Measures,* reunited her with director Michael Apted. They hadn't worked together in over a decade, since *Firstborn* in 1984. The film starred Hugh Grant and Gene Hackman and was a moderately suspenseful medical thriller that gave her little to do other than look earnest and determined. Sarah served as a medical assistant in this tale of a dedicated doctor who uncovers illegal medical practices in a big-city hospital. Her duplicitous character may or may not have had Grant's best interests at heart. *Extreme Measures* came and went rather quickly, and Sarah, critically, was barely noticed. And when she was, it was not necessarily complimentary. *Variety* offered the tepid assessment that "Sarah Jessica Parker has a part that functions almost totally as a plot device." The law of averages was that Sarah would come up against a situation like this. Her character was little more than window dressing, and her performance was easily dismissed as typically good but stuck in a vacuum of stock situations and little motivation. But the film offered her the opportunity to work with one of the consummate pros in Gene Hackman and to reacquaint herself with Hugh Grant.

It was during this period that Sarah returned to familiar territory when she re-created her role of Sarah Geldhart in the film version of the 1991 play *The Substance of Fire.* Ever the perfectionist, Sarah thought that with the movie she had finally done the character justice. The nature of film served to open up the range of emotions. Sarah obliged with a taut performance that, despite the film's limited release and minuscule box office success, served to remind audiences that the actress was first rate. The filming of *The Substance of Fire* was an intense, often claustrophobic exercise of almost endless takes. Sarah acquitted herself quite well in a small but effective part opposite an experienced cast that included Timothy Hutton, star of such megahits as *Ordinary People* (1980) and *French Kiss* (1995).

Sarah's fourth film of 1996 was a dark, very New York comedy, *If Lucy Fell.* In it, Sarah played a young woman (Lucy) struggling in affairs of the heart who makes a pact with her equally frustrated male friend (Joe, played by the film's writer-director, Eric

Schaeffer) that, if neither of them finds true love by the age of 30, they will meet at the Brooklyn Bridge and jump off. The story behind the story proved to be almost as good. Eight years earlier, Eric Schaeffer was struggling to make ends meet by driving a cab when he happened to pick Sarah up as a fare. In 1995, Schaeffer, who had long since given up driving a cab, once again met Sarah at a mutual friend's birthday party. He asked her to read the script for *If Lucy Fell*. She was interested but not totally convinced. Schaeffer waged a consistent campaign to woo her, going so far as to take her chicken soup when she was sick. Eventually, she agreed to do the film.

At that point, *If Lucy Fell* was still an independent film without any big-studio support. But word about the quality of the script was getting around, and, when Ben Stiller agreed to play a secondary role in the film as a dreadlocked artist who touches Sarah's heart, TriStar Films agreed to back and distribute the film. Things changed overnight. The budget increased, and so did the memos from the studio executives. Sarah was concerned that the film had suddenly become bigger than the ability of Schaeffer to bring it together.

There was some talk that Sarah was beginning to waver on doing the film. But how could she say no to the man who had brought her chicken soup? Sarah's enthusiasm for the project resulted in her turning in a wonderfully nuanced performance. With the addition of Stiller, portions of the film began to take on a highly improvisational feel. However, Sarah persisted in acting her way, focusing on what was needed and usually nailing her scenes almost immediately. That occasionally put her in conflict with Schaeffer, who admitted that he was still insecure and needed numerous takes to get one good one. Sarah did not always agree with him, but since he was the director she went along with his decisions. The upside continued to be Sarah's mastery of the comedic form. "She has grace and a wonderful sense of physical humor," remembered Schaeffer. "Smart New Yorky humor in a great package." In a showcase of her deeply ingrained New York attitudes, Sarah achieved a smooth mix of comedy and real-world

STEVE SANDS / CORBIS OUTLINE

Sarah on the set of *If Lucy Fell*

pathos. In striking contrast to previous performances, there was a real sense of urgency and believable edgy emotion attached to her performance. *If Lucy Fell* is not a film normally held up as one of her best performances, but it is definitely one of her more fully realized portrayals.

The movie opened to mixed and often dismissive reviews, but Sarah managed to gather no small amount of critical applause, as well as the occasional criticism, for her efforts. The *New York Times* said, "Ms. Parker is straining her adorableness to the limit." The *Boston Globe* took a different view: "Parker impresses repeatedly with her rueful looks." *New York* magazine said, "Sarah Jessica Parker is something to see. She's developed an ingratiating comic style." *Variety* lauded Sarah by saying, "The veracity she offers is ferocious and infectious."

Sarah had carefully planned her schedule for 1996. It was grueling, with no conflicts or overlaps between projects, but she had very little time off. She barely had time to take a breath after completing *If Lucy Fell*. She was reunited with her *Ed Wood* director Tim Burton for the science fiction madness of *Mars Attacks!*, an all-star bit of craziness and pulp attitudes based on a popular, grizzly set of trading cards. Burton thought she was perfect for the character Nathalie Lake and cast her without auditions. Sarah had no illusions about her role as a doomed talk-show host. The monsters and the special effects were the real stars of the film, and she was there to look good and, like most of the big names who eagerly climbed on board, to ultimately die horri-bly. She looked at it as a paid vacation. And it was a lucrative "holiday," too, because by this time Sarah was making between one and four million dollars per picture.

But she would also look back upon working with a director of Tim Burton's talent and temperament as a truly educational experience. She enhanced her skills in the sequences in which she had to play off special effects, and, in playing opposite the likes of Jack Nicholson and Pierce Brosnan, she could not help but enlarge her acting perspective. But *Mars Attacks!* was simply an excuse to play.

As was always the case with a Tim Burton film, reviewers were ready to either praise or slam it. The extent to which Parker's performance was noticed is best typified by the *People* review: "It tells you something that the highlight of this alleged satire is when an alien prankster grafts Parker's head onto the body of a Chihua-hua." But some reviewers were straightforward in their reviews of the actress. *Drama-logue* said that "Sarah Jessica Parker is full of bounce." The *Sacramento Bee* critic stated, "Sarah Jessica Parker gets all the funniest lines and situations." And, despite the all-star ensemble, *Entertainment Today* announced that "Sarah Jessica Parker comes close to stealing the show."

How to Succeed in Marriage 7

During much of Sarah's rush of film work Matthew was on the west coast in a production of *How to Succeed in Business without Really Trying*. The musical was a revival of the 1960s Broadway hit, which had starred Robert Morris. Coincidentally, both Morris and Matthew won Tony Awards for their portrayals of J. Pierpont Finch, the ambitious window cleaner who rises to the top of the business world. Sarah gushed in pride when Matthew walked off the stage with the 1995 Tony for Best Performance by a Leading Actor in a Musical, 33 years after the original victory! The production relocated to New York, where it was having continued success. Matthew was joined by actress Megan Mullally, who went on to costar in the hit TV series *Will and Grace*.

Immediately, there was talk that it would be a real great marketing ploy if Sarah would join Broderick in the musical's New York run in the role of Rosemary. The couple had a good laugh at the notion at first. But when the talks turned serious, they foresaw some real obstacles. Would they have any chemistry on stage? Could Sarah, who had not sung since her 1978 run in *Annie*, carry off the musical numbers? And, possibly worst of all, would there be creative differences? Sarah, in a *New York Times* interview, did not think so. "I can't imagine fighting with any actor about anything, and certainly not with Matthew. I'd rather have him as a boyfriend than fight about whether I upstage him or not. I'll be happy to be upstaged."

Eventually, Sarah decided that playing opposite her boyfriend was not a good idea. "It seemed like it should be Matthew's show," she offered to the *Christian Science Monitor*. "The two of us shouldn't be terrified at the same time." Which was fine with Broderick, who remained cautious in his comments to the *New York Times*. "The part that takes some adjusting and is a little uncomfortable for me is I have a slight feeling of dangling our couplehood around Times Square."

But halfway through the musical's run, and after some long conversations between the couple, Sarah decided to give it a try. Of course, there was the matter of not having sung on stage in 16 years. Sarah solved that problem with a quick trip to Los Angeles, where she had a crash course in singing with a cantor. During rehearsals, whatever lingering doubts Matthew may have had disappeared, and he agreed that Sarah was very right for the part and that the chemistry between them on stage was quite good. His feeling was reflected in the positive reviews that greeted their run on Broadway.

Encouraged by the success of *How to Succeed in Business without Really Trying*, Sarah moved on to another musical, *Once upon a Mattress*, based on the Hans Christian Andersen fairy tale *The Princess and the Pea*. Although a bouncy, well-spirited, and just-right-for-the-kids play, *Once upon a Mattress* had always been considered a slight production with physical demands that could make life difficult for an actress attempting the role. The play's music was written by Mary Rogers, daughter of Broadway legend Richard Rogers—*Oklahoma!* (1955), *South Pacific* (1956), *Sound of Music* (1965), and so on—and the original opened at the Phoenix Theatre on Broadway on May 11, 1959, starring Carol Burnett. It ran for 460 performances, and Burnett is considered a role model for all who came after. Sarah, wanting to stay in New York, thought it was the perfect vehicle. Her reemerging singing skills and her ability to carry a play were much in evidence on opening night, although reviewers did not take too kindly to the performance.

The cloud hanging over *Once upon a Mattress* enlarged when a feud developed between the production's director, Gerald Gutierrez, and the show's writer-lyricist, Marshall Barer, that resulted in Barer being barred from the theater. The show's producer, Michael David, indicated that Barer had been a destructive force during the rehearsal process, and that was the reason for his not being allowed in the theater. It was later revealed that the problem, at least as Barer saw it, centered on Sarah. Barer told the *New York Daily News* that he was barred from the theater after he offered to help Sarah with her performance. "Sarah was having trouble and I reached out to her. I told her that I had some tapes of Carol Burnett [in the original production] and that there is much that she could learn from them. When Gerry found out, he banished me." Barer indicated that Sarah's voice was not up to the demands of the show, but he was countered by a production assistant who talked to the *New York Daily News* on the condition of anonymity. "They banned Marshall because, after the first preview, he barged backstage and said, 'This show is a disaster and you [Sarah] are a disaster! I'm going to sit down and make you watch [the tape] of Carol Burnett and you are going to imitate her exactly!'"

What had started out as a fun job for Sarah turned into a minefield of accusations and personal attacks. The producers seriously considered canceling the play. Rumors abounded. One was that Sarah, upset at the problems, was considering leaving the show. Another had the producers delicately negotiating with Sarah to have her leave quietly. There was no truth to any of these, and those close to the situation reported that Sarah stood her ground amid the chaos and steadfastly refused to bow out. Sarah would not comment on the behind-the-scenes conflict, but it would be safe to say that the tension ultimately hurt her performance, especially when Barer, in a parting shot to the *New York Daily News*, dismissed the production of his work as a loser. But good word of mouth overcame the mediocre reviews and the backstage intrigue and resulted in *Once upon a Mattress* having a six-month run in front of packed houses.

Sarah was candid in admitting that the workload in 1996 was "psychotic," but her insecurity about work prevented her from saying no to offers. In hindsight, she wished she had said no to *Once upon a Mattress*. "Sometimes opportunities look better on paper," she lamented in *Harpers Bazaar*. "When I did *Once upon a Mattress*, I needed to focus a little. I never considered that it wouldn't turn out well. Had I known, I would have said, 'I'll take a big, bad movie instead.'"

However, her negative feelings regarding the play did not get in the way of her basic decency. Anne Brown, another actor in the *Once upon a Mattress* production, remembered that Sarah would always bring doughnuts for the other cast members. One day, when Brown's children were in the audience, Sarah invited them backstage and made a big fuss over them and complimented their mother's performance. And no matter how tired she was after the physically demanding performance, she would linger by the stage door, signing autographs and talking to the children who made up a large majority of the audience.

Ever the perfectionist, Parker had to admit she was overworked during the run of *Once upon a Mattress*. Years later, she would tell *Redbook* that 1996 was a lot more arduous than she had ever let on at the time. "You can't do four movies and be good to everybody and be flying all night and shooting all day with a different wig and then singing on Broadway without feeling tired. You endlessly feel you're letting someone down."

Despite all the behind-the-scenes drama, Sarah managed to acquit herself quite well in a role that required a lot. She was more than up to the physical requirements of the show. And despite all the distractions centered on her singing ability, she delivered a capable if not spectacular performance. Her strengths as an actor, in particular her strong ties to the theater tradition, were the best element of her performance, rich in substance and fine-tuned to the tone and scope of the play. And while reviewers were divided on the relative worth of this production of *Once upon a Mattress*, they generally agreed that Sarah was the best thing about it. The

New Leader, in a near-rave review, stated, "The star can carry a tune around the stage, dance and whirl and pratfall without pausing to catch her breath and can wring comedy out of a stone. Parker doesn't mind making a fool of herself in the pursuit of laughter." *Backstage* echoed those sentiments: "Parker does remarkably well as Princess Winnifred, playing her like an overzealous good time gal." The *New York Post* gushed, "To see the ever-enchanting Sarah Jessica Parker light up a stage is a joy," while *Associated Press* praised the actress by stating, "Parker is a delightful comedian." In the end, *Once upon a Mattress* proved to be a valuable object lesson to Sarah. Rather than taking an offer at face value, from now on she would check all elements of a project and the individuals involved. The frustration and bad feelings would disappear after a time. But she would not make the same mistake again.

The good personal reviews easily overcame the tensions and added to the feeling that Sarah was ending the year on a high note. Through a wide array of acting challenges, she had cemented her reputation as a topflight actress. Yet the career choices she was making continued to raise barriers to her achieving A-list recognition. But Sarah could not complain, because her choices were keeping things exciting, which, she would often explain, was the goal of any real actor.

Living in a pure acting environment was a constant source of strength for her as her career grew. If it was not for her strong ties to the theater and her insistence on doing only good work, Sarah could have easily fallen into the morass of faceless actors who will do anything and ultimately end up doing nothing but paying the rent. "In the theater, you're not scrutinized to the degree that you are in television and film," she reported in *Redbook.* "You're not being paid an exorbitant, obscene amount of money. You're not being waited on hand and foot. Cute, precious behavior is not coddled. It's primarily about the work." But, as she noted in an *Independent Online* interview, she was grateful for her opportunities in film. "Film subsidizes my love for the theater. And it's fortuitous that my film experiences aren't just for income reasons. They often can be really enjoyable, creative, and interesting and challenging, as well as providing a nice, healthy income."

Despite her denials, money was always a consideration in her career decisions. Sarah was not rich, but in a competitive climate, with erratic employment and income often averaging less than $5,000 a year, she was decidedly comfortable with her lucrative film projects. Consequently, the choices to work or not were finally hers. With good roles coming her way, she was becoming much more particular in the projects she picked. While she would look at anything in which the character resembled her work in L.A. Story, she would pass on imitation or exploitation. There was also much in the offerings that reflected her cult status in movies like Ed Wood. For Sarah, the two main criteria remained unchanged. How good was the story, and would the character ring true and be something other than window dressing? It was becoming much easier for Sarah to say no to the fluff and yes to the good stuff.

Personally, the love between Sarah and Matthew had grown even stronger in their four years together. There was never any doubt that they would be together forever. But while Sarah had never had any problem with cohabiting without being married, she was still conscious of her mother's traditional views, and she decided that she could not be like so many of her celebrity peers who were having children without the benefit of a formal marriage. Sarah had never considered that kind of arrangement and never would. Being a single mother was not an attractive lifestyle, and she was too honest a person to even think of getting pregnant in order to trap Matthew into marriage.

Sarah believed and that she would have her happy ending with the man she loved. The only thing left was to make it all official. Sarah had deliberately stopped talking about marriage and children with Matthew. She had long ago learned that he did not like being pushed into a corner and would make his decision in his own time. Well, Sarah was patient. She could wait.

If Sarah regretted one thing about her desire to get married, it

The happy couple

was that she had made it public. She was still mortified about her outburst on *Letterman,* and in looking back she felt calculating and desperate, two sides of her personality she did not like too much. "I had no interest in holding a gun to someone's head so he'd walk down the aisle to me," she said in a candid *Redbook* interview. "I wanted to be happily married because he [Matthew] wanted to be married." The topic would inevitably come up when Sarah chatted to her mother or her brothers and sisters. Toby, in particular, must have felt odd about the situation since he had introduced Sarah and Matthew and had made it possible for them to get together. All Sarah could say to inquiring minds was that it had not happened yet. And although it was often speculated that she suffered in silence at Matthew's inability to commit to marriage, there was never a doubt that she would stick with him no matter what the circumstances, because she was that much in love. She also did not want what had happened to her mother to happen to her. Sarah had suffered through enough of the chaos caused by her parents' divorce. She was anxious to live her fairy-tale fantasy of everlasting love and marriage, but she did not want to force an uncomfortable situation on Matthew. She believed he would commit at some point, and she was willing to wait.

And so the emotional stalemate continued. Matthew's personality, as she had discovered over the course of their live-in relationship, was very much in sync with hers. He could be effusive and funny, even at times when she least expected him to be. He also had the shyness and simplicity of a little boy at other times, and Sarah found that lovable. It didn't hurt that his studious good looks and subtle mannerisms had been an instant turn-on to her. But what Sarah would claim had ultimately sealed the relationship for her was his serious, no-nonsense nature that would surface in his wit, his intelligence, his dedication, and his persistence in even the most mundane matters. With Matthew, there was rarely a surprise and a whole lot of stick-to-itiveness that, for Sarah, spelled love and reliability, two things that she placed great stock in after observing her mother's two marriages.

Yet the never-ending marriage speculation was becoming an

annoyance to the couple's friends, who had been standing by them for going on four years, waiting for what they assumed would be Matthew's proposal. It was frustrating because they knew the couple were meant for each other. Close friend Don Shankman laughingly told *People*, "It's as if all her friends were standing beside her, thinking, 'What are you gonna do, bud?'"

Matthew, who had always held the door tightly shut when it came to discussing personal matters, did let his guard slip during an interview with *E! Online*. He readily admitted that, while he loved Sarah, the idea of a ring and a formal commitment had never really meant that much to him. He also explained that he was uncomfortable with the constant speculation and questioning about if and when Sarah and he would get married. "It was very unpleasant. It's in some ways my fault. I never really knew how not to talk about being in a relationship. It's hard to talk a little about it because then people want to know everything. It's very bizarre to have strangers say, 'So, when are you getting married?' I'd find myself getting into a discussion with the subway token clerk about marriage."

What Sarah did not know was that, behind the smokescreen of indecision, Matthew had been thinking long and hard about marriage. Logically, he could not think of a reason not to. He loved her with all his heart. She was the one he wanted to spend the rest of his life with. She was the woman he wanted to bear his children. The wheels were slowly beginning to turn. What Sarah did not know was that the wheels were slowly tipping in the direction of yes.

So Sarah was caught completely by surprise when, right in the middle of their run in *How to Succeed in Business without Really Trying*, Matthew proposed. While Sarah remained quiet on the particulars of the proposal, it was likely the simple romantic moment that she summed up when she said, "He asked and I was delighted." There. Over and done with. Proposal made. Proposal accepted. Now came the hard part. The couple were instantly caught in the flood of emotions that goes along with making that kind of decision. All of a sudden, the idea of making their union legal was a scary proposition. They both had prewedding jitters, but they both thought it was a life-affirming moment. They both felt ready.

Given their long-held attitude toward the press and privacy, they agreed to keep their coming nuptials a secret. They told only a handful of close family members and friends that May 19, 1997, was the date they had chosen. "We really didn't want it [our wedding] to be about strangers," Sarah said in an *E! Online* interview after the fact. "We both come from pretty large families, and we wanted our wedding to be for them. It didn't feel appropriate to invite a photographer or any press to something that meant so much to us."

The location of the wedding would be disclosed only the day before it took place, partly because they hadn't found a location yet. This was fantasy come true, so an ordinary church service would simply not do. Sarah was looking for her version of a fairy-tale palace in which the wedding ceremony would take place. At one point, she thought she had found the ideal place in an old Greenwich Village townhouse that was empty and for sale. But that didn't work out. Sarah kept looking and eventually found the perfect place in the very old, very run-down Angel Oresanz Synagogue on the Lower East Side. The congregation had long since abandoned the building. On the surface, it seemed to be an odd choice. The paint was peeling, there were unsightly cracks in the walls and ceiling, and the building, originally built in 1850, had obviously seen better days. But Sarah could see beyond these deficiencies. It was a mystical place. She saw the tradition and history in the raised podium area and the balconies that overlooked the main room of the synagogue. And, although she was not formally religious, she was proud of her Jewish roots. Like Sarah, Matthew was half-Jewish. Her plan had always been to hold the wedding amid the flickering light and shadows of candlelight. And this synagogue, without electricity, would be the perfect place.

Sarah's choice of venue was fine with Matthew, as was just about any other one, because, although he had definite ideas about certain elements of the wedding such as the wording of the invitation, he was pretty much letting Sarah make most of the decisions. Knowing Matthew to be stubborn when he wanted his way, Sarah had started making the wedding plans expecting a lot of friction, but she would tell her friends that she was pleasantly surprised that Matthew was so agreeable.

As the big day drew closer, the couple found themselves going to greater and greater lengths to keep their secret from the prying eyes of the press. When it came time for Sarah and Matthew to register for wedding gifts, they used fake names. They were also forced to juggle wedding plans with Sarah's role in *Once upon a Mattress*. However, despite their best efforts, rumors had begun to spread. Paparazzi began camping outside the couple's apartment in an attempt to get the all-important photos of the two of them leaving for the wedding. Those shots had suddenly become a valuable commodity for the always celebrity-hungry tabloids. Reporters from both the mainstream and the tabloid press began calling members of Sarah's and Matthew's families, and one reporter even pretended to be a FedEx delivery man. Eventually, a reporter from *E! Online* managed to get Sarah's unlisted telephone number and badgered the couple about their wedding plans. The couple did their best to deflect the questions. Just days before the wedding, Matthew told a reporter, "These stories seem to come in waves. You think people would be bored with them by now. They're never true."

Sarah and Matthew were soon bombarded with telephone calls at all hours of the day and night, which did nothing for their prewedding jitters. Many of the calls were from well-wishers calling to congratulate the couple. Others were from reporters who wanted a scoop. They did their best to deny that they were getting married, but one night they finally realized their big secret was out when Sarah met Matthew outside their apartment to go to dinner. "There were people looking through our garbage," she recalled to *E! Online*. "So it was out. We don't flatter ourselves that we're that interesting. It must have been a slow news week." With visions of an army of photographers dogging their path on the day of the wedding, the couple turned to their friends for help. They spent the night before the wedding at the home of actor Ron Rifkin, who had worked with Sarah in the play *The Substance of Fire*. Another friend went to the couple's apartment to pick up the things they would need for the wedding and literally walked in and out of the building in front of a group of paparazzi. The day before the wedding, a select group of family and friends were called with the invitation, which, to confuse things even more, did not even mention a wedding. Sarah's friend Kathleen Reinmann told *USA Today* that they were only told to go to New York for a party. Needless to say, guests arriving at the synagogue were shocked to discover that the party was actually the wedding of Sarah Jessica Parker and Matthew Broderick.

The deception worked. On May 19, 1997, an estimated 140 family members and friends gathered in the synagogue, amid flickering candlelight, as Matthew and Sarah became husband and wife in a short, fairly secular ceremony officiated by Matthew's sister, an Episcopal minister. The bride wore black, the consensus of those in attendance being that it was a sign that Sarah was a true New Yorker. True to his unpretentious nature, Matthew wore a simple dark suit rather than a tuxedo.

The party after the ceremony had an added bit of intrigue when it was discovered that a photographer for the *National Enquirer* had somehow sneaked into the affair and had been snapping pictures. But before long, the man was caught and his film confiscated.

The party was a fantasy-filled gala. The famed Peter Duchin orchestra played big band, Broadway show tunes, and jazz. Tunes like "Someone to Watch Over Me" and "Love and Marriage" kept the revelers singing and dancing the night away. Sarah and Matthew laughingly told their guests that they were still getting used to the idea of referring to each other as husband and wife. The toasts and good wishes were numerous. The food was excellent. Parker would later acknowledge that it was the wedding that she had been dreaming of.

Word had quickly spread around town about the celebrity wedding, and by 2 a.m., when the party was winding down, an army of photographers had arrived and were camped outside, waiting to snap the happy couple as they embarked on their honeymoon. With the help of friends, Sarah and Matthew once again managed to avoid the paparazzi by sneaking out a side door.

As for the honeymoon, there would not be one, at least not immediately, because Sarah had to be back at work the next day for a matinee performance of *Once upon a Mattress*, and Matthew, had to report to the New York set for his starring role in the movie *Godzilla*. But the lack of a traditional honeymoon could not dampen Sarah's joy at having a lifelong dream finally come true. "This is a very special night," she would later exclaim.

With Matthew working long hours and *Once upon a Mattress* drawing to the end of its run, Sarah felt no compunction to take time off. However, her mood dictated that, whatever she did, it should not be heavy. Her next film was the romantic comedy *'Til There Was You*, in which she was cast as Taffy, the washed-up and cynical former child actor. On the surface, the character seemed to be comic relief. But the film's director, Scott Winant, respected Sarah too much to simply waste her in a paper-thin role and went to great lengths to explain that there was a lot more going on with Taffy. "Outwardly, she looks like comedic relief," he explained to the *Los Angeles Times*. "But the whole point was to show [that] this character has weight and consequence. By the end of the movie, we care deeply for her." Winant's prediction that Sarah's role would be substantial was accurate. The romance between the characters played by Dylan McDermott and Jeanne Tripplehorn was a fairly stock story line. Sarah's over-the-hill child star was literally the center of attention and would steal every scene she was in. Whether by design or luck, Sarah had the best lines and the most interesting scenes in the film.

The fact that she was able to invest some life and depth into what could have easily been an inconsequential outing proved her ability to mold any role into something special. In fact, the audience is drawn into her character and ends up wishing that more of the film could have been devoted to her story. Unfortunately, critics were not kind to *'Til There Was You*, dismissing it as, among other things, a lightweight cross between Jerry Seinfeld and Woody Allen. But even as they dismissed the film, the critics tended to recognize what Sarah had brought to it. *Entertainment Weekly* described her as "Radiantly narcissistic," providing "the movie's only perky moments." *Variety* acknowledged that she was "the only performer given her due and some range." Sarah had long felt confident that she could play any role she was given. But it was rare when critics acknowledged that her work, although basically secondary to the film's story line, was the sole reason for seeing a movie. However, Sarah felt bad that the movie had not done better and would continue to defend it as a solid, albeit flawed, film. She was occasionally torn by such proclamations. Ever the perfectionist, she was appreciative that she was being recognized as a talented performer, but she was getting a bit weary of having her performances be the shining moments in somewhat dull films. However, she reasoned that she could only do her best with any given project and that, eventually, all the pieces would come together.

Sarah and Matthew's wedding rekindled the media speculation that the couple would soon begin trying to have a baby. And unlike many modern-day actresses who have managed to balance motherhood and a career, Sarah was clear that, when they decided to have children, her career would instantly become secondary. And the implication was that, when that time did come, Sarah would not miss the celebrity life and the acclaim. "When you're a mom, you're totally famous to your kids," she insisted in a *Redbook* interview. "And that sounds just fine by me."

The Prim Princess Does Sex

8

On January 1, 1997, Sarah made a New Year's resolution to stop using the F word. She also vowed that she would give up smoking. She promised to break an age-old habit of biting the inside of her cheek and almost immediately backslid on that one. And finally she renewed her vow not to do on-screen nudity. And then along came *Sex and the City*, which immediately threatened the longevity of at least two of the remaining three resolutions.

The portrayal of sex on television had come a long way since the buttoned-down, separate-bed days of the 1950s. The way had been paved in the mid-1960s by *Peyton Place*, which had scalded viewers' sensibilities with its then-frank sexual acting out. In the 1980s, *Dallas* ushered in a new era of scandal and bed-hopping and a stretching of the boundaries of what could be seen on the small screen. In the 1990s, everything from *Beverly Hills, 90210* to the sizzling trash of *Melrose Place* defined a new frankness in what could be said and seen on television. There remained only one way for sex on television to take the next logical step: *Sex and the City*.

Darren Star had worked on prime-time network trash as a screenwriter and producer with *Melrose Place, Beverly Hills, 90210*, and the short-lived and obviously sexual *Central Park West*, starring Raquel Welch. But he was finding the ever-increasing conservatism of the networks an obstacle to getting anything new

125

or even remotely controversial off the ground. And so, when he optioned Candace Bushnell's racy book about four thirtysomething women and their sexual adventures and misadventures in New York City, *Sex and the City*, he knew the only chance to get it on the air and done right was to go to cable. HBO, already a leader in cutting-edge, adult entertainment, loved the idea and commissioned a pilot with a back door to 11 additional episodes. "I thought if [HBO executives] look at me and say, 'You gotta be kidding, we're never doing this,' then I'm in trouble," Star told *TV Guide*. "But HBO got the joke."

Casting the city of New York as the backdrop to the show was easy. Star knew that the tough part would be getting his actresses. He also knew that *Sex and the City* would be a risky proposition for any actress. As conceived by the producer, the show would be rated a hard R, replete with profanity, on-screen sexuality with varying degrees of nudity, and alternately cynical and hopeful takes on the mating game.

Integral to the story is the character of Carrie Bradshaw, who writes a sex column for a New York publication and often incorporates her experiences and those of her three single girlfriends into her work. Based on these experiences, the stories would not only titillate in their frankness but also be totally relevant to women and possibly men. Given those parameters, the actress who played Carrie would have to walk a fine line. In Star's mind, Carrie had to possess the brains of Dorothy Parker and the body of Marilyn Monroe. He had passed on the usual array of late teen and young adult stars, many of whom had the obvious physical attributes but could not begin to project the required intellect and sass. Then he thought of Sarah Jessica Parker. "Sarah Jessica has the biting wit I wanted the character to have," Star told *People*. "But she is also sympathetic. You really need the right person to make an imperfect character likable." But given her reputation as somebody with a conservative bent and her largely innocent on-screen image, he knew getting her to agree would not be easy. And so the producer approached Sarah with a rare

The women of *Sex and the City*

offer. She would serve as one of the show's producers (uncredited during the first season) as well as be the star of the show.

The timing for such a proposal could not have been better for Sarah. By the late 1990s, the general impression was that her career had plateaued. She had proven a solid talent as a support character in major films and had more than enough talent to carry off the lead in small, eccentric productions. But, despite her ongoing insistence that her career was right where she wanted it to be, she had not yet reached superstardom. Although it was a risky project, *Sex and the City*, if done right, could be exactly what Sarah needed to take the next giant step.

Sarah responded to the offer with intrigue and nervousness. That the show would be shot entirely in New York meant she could go home at night. And with Matthew's current work in films and the theater keeping him in the city, she wanted to be home as much as possible. She liked the idea that *Sex and the City* was under the HBO banner and that the reins of censorship would not be so tight. A lot of her concerns were not with the show or the subject matter but with what the possibility of a weekly series would do to her personal and professional lives. Part of her fear was that everything would change. The idea that she would be in people's homes on a regular basis and consequently much more recognizable was a major concern. She and Matthew had spent years guarding their privacy and cultivating a personal lifestyle that would allow them to pass easily through the public eye. She did not want that to change. "The question was whether I wanted to do a television series at all," she said in a *Zap2 It.com* interview. "I was scared of that kind of commitment and the idea that I might not be able to do anything else." Star acknowledged that her concerns were not unfounded. "I was very reticent for lots of reasons to do a television show," she told *TNT*, "and he sort of threw me a bone. He said, 'Look, you could learn a lot. It could really be a great experience and you could learn a lot about what it takes to shoot a series in New York City.' And so I said, 'Well, that sounds good.'"

Of course, the idea that her character would be hopping in

and out of bed with other men was another concern. Matthew had always been comfortable with Sarah being in romantic situations with leading men in her movies. But *Sex and the City* was an R-rated show. Happily, Sarah discovered that her husband was an even more highly evolved human being than she had thought and that he had no problem with her doing the show. And, in fact, it was at the urging of Matthew, along with her brother Pippen, that she accepted the offer.

But with the development of the show moving along at a leisurely pace, Sarah found the opportunity to do a couple of off-beat projects that appealed to her on a more spiritual level. Her interest in her Jewish roots and her curiosity about her cultural background got her involved in these enterprises. She appeared as a guest star on the Jewish-themed educational children's show *Shalom Sesame* and, with Leonard Nimoy, narrated the stirring documentary *A Life Apart: Hasidism in America*.

When she returned to *Sex and the City*, Sarah was admittedly startled when she read the first few scripts. Nothing Star had told her about *Sex and the City* had prepared her for the scenes in which Carrie casually uttered four-letter words. And there was that scene at the end of the pilot script that called for Carrie's breasts to appear in silhouette. "Oh God, the scripts are salty and ribald," Sarah related in the *New York Times*. "This is something I've never done before." Sarah took a step back. In another time and under different circumstances, she might have bolted from the series. But she loved the basic premise. She just thought her part needed a bit of fine-tuning. Sarah was quick to tell Star about her problem with nudity and her reluctance to swear, even if both elements seemed to fit logically into the *Sex and the City* premise. Star and the writers restructured the scripts to accommodate her admitted prudish side. She would be seen in bed and in various states of undress but never completely nude. The profanity was trimmed back, and the offensive F-word was all but eliminated. Sarah was now quite happy.

But her control was not total. She related to the *Richmond News Tribune* that, "If something is really vulgar, I have conversations with the writers where I say I'm not comfortable with that. It doesn't mean they'll make the change, but we do discuss it." One early story line involved Carrie's diaphragm getting stuck and her seeking help from her friends to remove it. Sarah confronted the writer about the implausibility of the situation, only to be told that it had actually happened to a friend of hers. Case closed.

Key to the success of the series was the chemistry that Sarah would have with her on-screen girlfriends. The casting process was a long and often tedious affair in which literally hundreds of actresses auditioned. For Sarah, this was a worrisome situation. Whomever was chosen would be in her life literally every day for several months and, if the show was a success, possibly several years. If their personalities did not mesh, *Sex and the City* could very easily become a nightmare. She was thrilled when the final choices were the actresses Kim Cattrall, Kristin Davis, and her old friend Cynthia Nixon, with whom she had worked on *My Body, My Child* in 1982. All three had extensive acting backgrounds, including some theater experience, which pleased Sarah. During the rehearsal stage, the four women immediately bonded and could regularly be found laughing and discussing the scripts and essentially acting like their characters on the show. And that, reasoned the producers, would be a key to the ultimate success or failure of the show. Because, from its inception, *Sex and the City* was far from normal sitcom fare—the frankness would be far ahead of anything that television had ever attempted. The actresses not only had to be quite comfortable in their alter egos, but they also had to be comfortable with the dialogue and situations they would be involved in. Television audiences are not dumb. If there was a hint that scenes were being played on less than a realistic level, people would instantly tune out.

Once the show was fully cast, a potential schism between Sarah and her cast mates loomed. Her three costars had no problems with the nudity requirements, but they announced publicly that Sarah's no-nudity clause was also not a problem and that she should do only what she felt comfortable doing.

Once filming on the first 12 episodes began, Sarah was very

involved in the show. She could be counted on to arrive early, usually about 7 a.m., and would immediately confer with the director and other actors about any of the questions or conflicts that inevitably arose. Sarah soon gained a reputation as somebody who was sincerely interested in the welfare of the cast and crew. In a *People* article, Star mentioned that "We work really long hours on the show, and I think her first and foremost concern is making sure the crew is in good spirits. She treats them like a family. She really has a mothering instinct." Coproducer Michael Patrick King would often echo Star's feelings and offered that, when she was not busy being everybody's friend, her experience and talent were major driving forces early in the show. "When you need her to be a star, she's a star," King told *Redbook*. "She glimmers in front of the camera. She's a great combination of a million things. Very hip. Funny. Emotional."

Part of her achievement could be traced to Sarah's happy home life. Contrary to the doomsayers who had predicted that being married would destroy the relationship, the formal marriage of Sarah and Matthew strengthened their love for and commitment to each other. When he was not working, Matthew would occasionally head to the *Sex and the City* set for lunch. But he knew from experience that launching any new project, especially a groundbreaking television series, took a lot of time and concentration, so he was just happy to offer encouragement and support when she got home at night. In the midst of this crazy time, Matthew was Sarah's rock.

Just how good Sarah was going to be in *Sex and the City* became clear as the producers ran through the dailies of the first few episodes. What they found was that, despite being happily married, she played the single-woman character of Carrie very well. Their lead actress had this uncanny ability to get out of herself. And given the extreme nature of Carrie, they thought that watching Sarah go through this transformation would be an ongoing treat. They were also happy that the hoped-for chemistry between Sarah and the other actresses was obvious. The degrees of understanding, tolerance, compassion, and humor that punctuated the

The cast *Sex and the City* celebrate their Golden Globe
for Best Television Series—Comedy/Musical

scenes in which the four women would inevitably gather at their
favorite bar to talk about their love lives, men, and sex were price-
less. In those scenes in which Carrie was dealing with individual
friends, Sarah, true to form, was a chameleon, offering up just the
right amount of shading and attitude to accommodate and compliment each personality. Since the dialogue and the situations
were sexually frank, even the most liberal of the cast members
would eventually find something offensive. Kristin Davis had a
particular problem with an episode in which her boyfriend of the
moment asks for anal sex. She balked at the idea but eventually
agreed to do the scene, then called up her mother and warned
her not to watch that episode.

Sarah continued to be uncomfortable with profanity and, in
particular, the dreaded F-word, which had turned up regularly in
the first few scripts. The actor would laugh, turn red, and cover
her mouth during rehearsals when she was forced to use that
expletive or other profanities. Eventually, the writers fine-tuned
Sarah's dialogue, and, as the season progressed, the dreaded F-word

was usually replaced with the S-word or something more palatable for the actress. There had been some talk of alleviating her problem with profanity by eliminating completely the words she found offensive. But Sarah would not agree to that, knowing full well that, for Carrie Bradshaw to be believable, she had to occasionally have a foul mouth.

Sarah remained excited as the show began to unfold, but there was still trepidation about the magnitude of what she had signed on for. She could live with the hard work and the long hours because, in a creative sense, she knew they were paying off. However, she was admittedly nervous about the audience's response. "We were making [the show] in the blind," she explained to *Entertainment Tonight*. "We knew that the subject matter was provocative, but we had no point of reference."

Once the show's publicity department got cranking, though, it was not long before educating the public about *Sex and the City* began in earnest. Endless interviews, set visits by the press, and sneak previews of the pilot episode to the entertainment media confirmed that this was a show that could be done only on cable and that its content was not for the easily offended. Sarah had always enjoyed doing interviews and, with a project that she strongly believed in, was particularly enthusiastic.

Sex and the City premiered on June 6, 1998. The ratings, by cable standards, were outstanding, and the reviews, as expected, were all over the place — some applauding the series for its bravery in pushing the envelope of sexuality, and others blaming the show for helping to usher in the rapid decline of morality in Western civilization. But while critics often damned the show with faint praise, they invariably singled out Sarah for her portrayal of Carrie, by which the series would live or die. "Parker is appealing as always," lauded *People*. "Parker's presence provides a star quality," *Variety* noted.

As the first season of 12 episodes unfolded, *Sex and the City* turned into an unbridled hit, and Sarah was, in the eyes of many, now a bona fide star. After spending so many years in search of stardom, she now had mixed emotions. She was not going to lie and say she did not appreciate the accolades, but she was also aware that stardom could create problems. She did not want her name on everybody's lips, creating tensions and jealousies on the show. Which was why, true to her giving nature, Sarah was quick to spread the praise around. She emphasized that *Sex and the City* was essentially an ensemble cast and that the show would not work without everybody's contribution. She also gave the writers full credit for the biting dialogue and the real-world attitudes that had made the show a hit.

And those writers were enjoying season one with the creation of Carrie's first serious on-screen relationship with the mysterious man known only as Mr. Big, played by actor Chris Noth, who had starred in *Law & Order* from 1990 to 1995. The electricity between the two characters could hardly be contained, and that extended to Sarah's impression of the character and the actor. "He's ruined me for other men on the show in a lot of ways," Sarah told *Entertainment Weekly*. "He's a big, grown-up man, not a boy. There's a feminine quality about a lot of actors, where they're not men first, they're actors first and vain. But Chris Noth is just a guy. I simply love him."

But with the success of *Sex and the City* came the inevitable misunderstandings about the show and its characters. Some critics immediately saw the word "Sex" in the title and blindly accused the characters on the show of engaging in nothing more than rampant sex. The misunderstanding of the show's concept and its portrayal of women began to hit close to home for Sarah when Matthew was asked during a round of television talk-show appearances how he felt about seeing his wife jumping in and out of bed with strange men all the time. Sarah was always ready to point out that the characters on *Sex and the City* were having no more sex than the characters on other network shows and that, if the show was guilty of anything, it was of taking advantage of the freedom afforded by HBO to talk frankly about sex as it was in the 1990s. In a TNT *Rough Cut* interview, she was ready to correct the misconceptions about Carrie. "My character doesn't jump in and out of bed all the time. I don't take my clothes off. But it's like an idea [people have] rather than actually having seen or watched the show. I think the show has just touched a nerve and brought the topic sort of to the forefront of conversation."

The controversy surrounding *Sex and the City* succeeded in boosting ratings to an even higher level. And the result was exactly what Sarah had feared—loss of privacy. She and Matthew used to be able to move in relative anonymity through their Greenwich Village neighborhood. Now their travels were constantly interrupted by people approaching Sarah for her autograph, asking her strange and sometimes inane questions, and basically forgetting that she was Sarah and treating her exactly like Carrie. In response, Sarah would reiterate that Carrie was nothing like her and that, the deeper the show delved into her on-screen persona, the more differences she was finding. "I have never been part of a circle of friends like Carrie has," she explained to *Entertainment News Daily*. "My life has always been much less public. I've never been somebody that frequently experimented, and I didn't display the comfort with sexuality the same way she does." But when the inevitable comparisons were finished, Sarah always maintained that she was awed and fascinated by the character and that Carrie was great fun to play.

Sarah went through a wide range of responses to this sudden adulation. There was amusement, amazement, and a touch of concern at how big an impact *Sex and the City* was having on her career. There were usually two piles of scripts in the couple's home: one for Matthew and the other for Sarah. But admittedly, in the wake of *Sex and the City*'s breakout success, her pile was bigger. In response to the question of whether her success was having a negative effect on Matthew's perceived fragile actor's ego, she would tick off her husband's current projects and insist that the only reason Matthew had periods of not working was that he was just too picky. "Right now Matthew is in a beautiful time in his career," she remarked in a *Los Angeles Daily News* interview.

Some thought that the time was right for Sarah and Matthew to follow the lead of other celebrity couples and do a film together. Sarah acknowledged that Matthew and she talked about that possibility all the time but that, as yet, they had not found the right project. But in the same breath, she wondered how good an idea that actually was. "The thing I keep thinking is, do we really want to do this in front of the American public?" she explained to *Entertainment Weekly*. "And sometimes I think maybe we shouldn't, that it's too private, unless we're in a film where we're not playing opposite each other."

For Matthew, the hectic schedule of *Sex and the City* had caused some anxious moments. That actors do not work regular hours was a given, and he knew that television is particularly grueling. But it was a period of readjustment as Sarah would often leave the house at six in the morning, work until midnight or later, return home for a scant four hours of sleep, and then return to the set early the next morning. But ever the trooper, Matthew, in a *TV Guide Online* interview, was nothing but supportive. "I'm very happy for her and I'm proud of the show. She works incredibly hard on it. It's hard to see somebody work that hard, but she enjoys it."

And, as the first season indicated, she was quite good at it. Although letting the scripts dictate where her character went, Sarah proved quite good at filling in the emotional and personal traits of Carrie. She was, admittedly, a bit tentative at first, preferring to underplay rather than go dangerously over the top. This decision would prove to be the right one as her character gradually grew into the situations that came her way and thus came across as much more believable.

Not too surprisingly, *Sex and the City* was renewed for a second season of 18 episodes, which, continuing HBO's counterprogramming attitude, would begin airing in the summer. With a hiatus of nearly four months, Sarah, who turned 33 shortly before the debut of *Sex and the City*, began looking around for something to do. Initially, she looked for a theater project, but it was tough to fit in a run in a play, with its long rehearsal time, given the firm starting date for the second season of *Sex and the City*.

Given the months of 14-hour days and her hectic work in films and theater over the past three years, there were those who openly

Celebrating her Golden Globe for
Best Comedic Actress in a TV show

questioned why Sarah would want to work at all during her break from *Sex and the City*. And she had to admit that toiling through the first season of *Sex and the City* had left her physically and mentally exhausted. But rather than sit and rest, Sarah was driven to find something to occupy her time. She was compelled to work because of her fear of never getting another part if she turned anything down. As always, Matthew was busy, primarily with theater work during this period. She would often respond to the charges of overwork by saying that she simply loved to work and try different things. However, in her more candid moments, she would remark that her workaholic actions came, in large part, from her fear that her next part might be her last and that she did not want to turn around in 10 years and find herself a middle-aged actress who was suddenly unemployable. She told the European magazine *Aftonbladet TV*, "As an actress, you have a very tiny window, and it is shut a bit at a time, day by day. I don't have any illusions. I'm aware of who I am, what I look like, and what I have to offer."

The films she was offered at that point were all over the place. There was much in the offerings that played to her newfound identity of Carrie Bradshaw, but, while Sarah was looking to do a comedy, she was looking for something a bit lighter. She found the perfect vehicle in the role of Little Nell Fenwick in the live-action version of the classic 1960s Jay Ward cartoon *Dudley Do-Right*. Ward was also responsible for the *Rocky and Bullwinkle* TV series in the 1970s. And so, while she knew she needed a rest, she looked at *Dudley Do-Right* and director Hugh Wilson, who had guided her fortunes in *The First Wives Club*, as a vacation and readily accepted the offer. "The appeal was, as always, to do something different," reflected Sarah in the *New York Daily News*. "There are few opportunities for women to do comedy, and there are fewer opportunities for women to do slapstick comedy. It was simply fun, liberating, and a silly way to make a living."

Dudley Do-Right, written and directed by Hugh Wilson and costarring Brenden Fraser, was an easy ride. The dialogue was over the top, and the story line, physical shtick, and situations were cartoonish in the extreme. All that was required of Sarah was to abandon belief and follow her director's orders. In fact, the hardest thing Sarah had to remember was that, following a season as producer and star on *Sex and the City*, on this film she was only an actor. "It's hard to go back to acting," she confided in a *Daily News* interview. "It's like putting a gag on your mouth. But there is a time and place for everything, and I think I can separate the two."

Those looking for a groundbreaking performance from Sarah in *Dudley Do-Right* were in for a disappointment. While her instincts were right in terms of bringing a cartoon character to life, what she could ultimately do with Nell was limited, particularly since director Wilson wanted to play things larger than life. However, Sarah turned in far from a rote performance. She displayed a good sense of slapstick and broad comedy with her costar, borrowing from the sensibilities she displayed in *Ed Wood*, and turned in a solid if unspectacular performance.

The movie eventually came out to mixed reviews and meager box office results, and Sarah was likewise a victim of so-so notices. *Variety* said that "Parker camps coquettishly," and the *Hollywood Reporter* blasted Sarah when it said that she "looks lost a good deal of the time." The *Daily Breeze* observed, "Parker is wide eyed and easily astonished." Finally, the *New York Times* mentioned that "Jessica Parker twitters well as the lovely Nell."

With *Dudley Do-Right* in the can, Sarah enjoyed a few weeks of quiet time at home with Matthew. These were good times for Sarah. With her career now in high gear and much more being asked of her professionally, quiet times at home, cooking big dinners for her family and friends or just hanging out, reading the *New York Times*, or watching mindless television began to take on extra importance. Because the days of struggling, typecasting, and being passed over were now over, quiet times would almost certainly be rare.

The toughest part of being elevated to star status turned on the question of money. In the past few years, Sarah had become fairly comfortable financially. Her father had long ago impressed upon her that she would be set for life once she earned $8 million. Although she did not reveal how much she was actually worth, the consensus among Hollywood speculators was that Sarah was at least halfway to her goal by the time she started the second season of *Sex and the City*. With the new money came the opportunities that she was not always ready for. Sarah was investing her money in conservative stocks and tax-free bonds, and she could buy virtually anything she wanted, yet she would instinctively balk at the idea of spending a little more for a nice pair of shoes. She readily admitted that her attitude regarding her newfound wealth continued to be shaped by memories of her rough childhood. She also acknowledged that her frugal nature was part of her philosophy of looking toward the future. "I want my children to not have to think about money," she told *Aftonbladet TV*. "That means I have to be very careful with my financial decisions." But slowly she was realizing that the days of poverty were gone forever. In fact, for Sarah, this period in her life was a time of self-examination, and she was now able to look at her past life in a more even-handed, less emotional manner than she ever had before.

With the recent recurring problems of Robert Downey Jr. and the tragic death of John F. Kennedy Jr., the press began digging up her past relationships and coming to her for comment. Sarah was leery of anybody meddling in her past and would usually brush the questions aside. Yet she was thrilled at having finally become in the eyes of the public a fully realized, successful personality. "What has happened is extraordinary," she told the *New York Times*. "There is not a day that passes that I am not grateful for the windfall."

Sarah was also happy to see that Matthew's career was likewise taking a firmer hold in film. As she was preparing to return for the second season of *Sex and the City*, Matthew was appearing in the films *Election* and *Inspector Gadget*. He was also much in demand and had his pick of any number of projects. Being a stage person, he tended to favor Broadway work, looking on films as a lucrative way to support his theater habit.

The couple were mutually supportive, and that went a lot

further than just talking about their careers. Sarah's love for Matthew had a protective, almost motherly, quality, which may well have had its roots in the encouragement her mother gave her when she was growing up. The fact that her mother had been there for her performances and had encouraged every facet of her life and career had been important for her. And it was reflected in her relationship with Matthew. When he opened in the play *Night Must Fall* midway through 1999, Sarah juggled her already busy schedule to make sure she was in the audience for the first six shows to support her husband. Matthew reciprocated by encouraging Sarah whenever possible.

Sarah returned to *Sex and the City* reenergized. Which was a good thing. As befitting any breakout success, the questions were already being asked about whether a show that focused on love and sex could continue to be creative. And there was the constant battle of perception. Despite the fact that Carrie had by season's end entered a monogamous, although admittedly tenuous, relationship with the character Mr. Big, people still considered all the women on the show freewheeling and sexually loose.

The biggest personal challenge facing Sarah on *Sex and the City* was that people still had a hard time separating her from the character of Carrie. Complete strangers would regularly come up to the actress on the street and tell her about their sex lives or offer to show her what was in their purses. She was also getting the mixed signal that, although people loved the show, some were ashamed to admit that they tuned in.

Sarah was relearning the power of television. "I'd forgotten how many people have televisions in their home," she told the *Philadelphia Inquirer*. "Matthew and I were people who were sort of known. People had relationships with us through movies and theater. But [with] television, people become aggressively familiar. I don't mean that in a bad way. I don't mean they're violent or rude or mean or physical. They're really familiar because you're in their home and they connect with the show." Being the center of attention everywhere they went was something new for the notoriously private and reserved couple. They did their best to be

Palling around with Chris Noth

gracious, but Sarah candidly told the *Inquirer* that "There are times when you're just tired and you don't want to be polite. You just want to go on your way." What they were finding out was that going their own way was not always easy. "People say things to me they wouldn't have said even a year ago," she said to *Zap2It.com*. "Even when I'm on talk shows, it seems like open season to act very forward and talk in a particularly frank way. But I'm not the character I play, and I've had to remind some people of that. Someone used pretty vulgar language with me recently, thinking it was funny. I finally had to say, 'Hey! I'm a lady.'"

The rush of continued attention began to add a new dimension of stress in Sarah's already complicated life. She began cutting back on the number of interviews she would do. And she became increasingly impatient with interviewers who would ask the same questions she had heard a thousand times. But like all moods in Sarah's life, it did not last long, and she easily slid back into being enthusiastic about *Sex and the City*.

It was in times of intense scrutiny regarding the show and herself that Sarah turned inward and examined her own feelings about Carrie. She found that, while she admired Carrie and did not see her actions as immoral, there was a lot about her life and her views about sexuality that she did not agree with. But finally she found that Carrie was a character she could live with.

The second season of *Sex and the City* mirrored the first. HBO had been so happy with the first season that they it wanted 18 episodes for the second. Sarah was also being well compensated for her contributions, with a reported salary increase to $150,000 per episode. But could they top the almost unbelievable success of season one? The answer was not long in coming. The new stories were smarter, the shots taken against establishment ideals more barbed, and the sexuality a lot hotter. And while there were moments during the second season in which characters bared all, Sarah's Carrie Bradshaw continued to avoid nudity. For her part, Sarah was a dynamo both in front and behind the camera, and she had just as much pride in her producing acumen as in her acting skills. "It's nice to feel that you're part of something, that you aren't just an actor for hire," she said. "You have something at stake, and you have some responsibilities. It makes you care a lot more about those around you, their welfare, and the quality of the show and how it's received."

From a purely acting point of view, in the second season of *Sex and the City*, Sarah succeeded in rounding out her character and capturing the joy and torment of Carrie Bradshaw. And it is to her credit that the actress had proved a quick study. She had learned not to overplay the elements of pathos and to stop short of overt caricature. There was also a spirited sense of wonder surrounding the happier moments in Carrie's life. That fostered a sense of hope that often balanced the cynicism. Sarah had figured out what made the character of Carrie tick, and the result was a consistently polished, engaging performance.

It also seemed that the critics had finally begun to figure the show out. Reviewers still cited sexual frankness as an overriding reason to tune in to *Sex and the City*, but they were also realizing that the show was populated by well-drawn, complex characters whose antics mirrored the real world. Women's groups began to champion the series for opening up avenues of intelligent dialogue between women, and between women and men. The level of support from socially respected groups was particularly heartening to Sarah. Her hope had always been to create an entertaining show populated by believable characters. That it would also strike an emotional chord with people and project a lifestyle that many could relate to added to the joy of the actress, who was delighted that *Sex and the City* might, in some ways, be making a difference.

The high quality of the show and, in particular, Sarah's star performance as Carrie were recognized shortly after the completion of *Sex and the City*'s second season when the Emmy nominations included a nod to the show for Outstanding Comedy Series and to Sarah for Best Actress in a Comedy Series. Realistically, she thought that she and the show had little chance for an award, citing the fact that *Sex and the City* was still too cutting edge for much of the mainstream television audience. What she was hoping for was a night out with friends and a good after-show party. That neither she nor the show captured the top prize on Emmy night was only a slight disappointment—Helen Hunt won for *Mad about You*. Getting nominated was a real thrill. Sarah's prize was yet to come. Nominated for a Golden Globe Award, Sarah put on a brave face amid the speculation that she would remain an nominee once again. She was nervous as she and Matthew made plans to fly to Los Angeles to attend the award ceremony in January 2000. She spouted the usual clichés to the media about how getting the nomination was an award in itself, but deep down, she wanted to win.

She and Matthew sat in the audience trying to hide their apprehension—they were excited and scared at the same time. Shortly after the beginning of the show, the nominees for best comedic actress in a TV show were announced. Sarah smiled for the cameras, but her heart was really beating. Then the announcement came: "And the winner is . . . Sarah Jessica Parker!"

Her eyes went wide, but she just sat there stunned and disbelieving. It was a few moments before she realized that she wasn't dreaming and started toward the stage. There were hugs and kisses for Matthew, producer Darren Star, and her costars. Her acceptance speech reflected her surprise. She had never won anything, she stammered, and now this. She thanked everyone in the show and in her life.

Later, when *Sex and the City* won for best TV comedy, Darren Star and the others were halfway through their thank-yous before Sarah appeared. She had been backstage giving media interviews and had not heard the announcement. Twice in one night. It couldn't get much better than this! Sarah felt like Cinderella, the belle of the ball.

Patience Is Rewarded

9

Sarah Jessica Parker turned 35 during the hiatus of *Sex and the City*. And despite having to endure the good-natured jokes about wrinkles and crow's feet, for Sarah there really was not much of a downside to taking that next step toward middle age. In fact, the occasion of her 35th birthday was a time for Sarah to reflect on her blessings. She was the producer and star of one of the most critically acclaimed and ravenously watched shows on television. Her marriage to Matthew Broderick was almost too good to be true. Her parents, after years of struggle, had finally reached a point in their lives where they were materially comfortable. Her siblings had all grown up and had gone on to have happy, fulfilling lives. There was still the lingering desire to have children, but she was content to wait until she and Matthew were a little less wrapped up in their careers. In the meantime, the couple would make the most of the time they had together.

Both were big New York Yankees fans, and when the team was in town they could often be found in the bleachers. They preferred the cheap seats because they liked to keep a low profile. Sarah was such a big fan that the night Matthew was receiving the GQ Theater Man of the Year Award, she was standing backstage with a transistor radio plugged in her ear, excitedly relaying the game highlights to people.

147

After visiting with family and friends, Sarah continued to enjoy such things as in-line skating and cooking big, high-calorie dinners for invited guests. Sarah loved to eat, and Matthew would often marvel that she ate like a longshoreman but never gained an ounce. She liked the simple pleasures that life offered. And that she was having professional success only added to her satisfaction.

Sarah was at peace, but invariably it was a peace tinged with bubbling enthusiasm for what was around the next corner. She was continually looking at scripts and considering offers. As always, Matthew was a wonderful sounding board, and the couple would spend hours discussing the merits of certain projects. On a professional level, Matthew and Sarah were very much in sync, because of their similar outlooks. When a script was way out in left field, they would have a good laugh while tossing it on the reject pile. When a script was borderline, they would debate its relative merits vigorously for hours. Matthew could be very convincing and was always logical in his arguments, whereas it was the rare exchange in which Sarah did not come from a position of passion. Often they would agree to disagree, but the best discussions between the couple seemed to be the ones that ended up in a hard-fought draw. Personally, it was the same. They both knew the looks that said "Give me space" or "Let's talk." Did they argue? Sure, what couple doesn't? But they rarely got angry, and they never stayed that way long—they both liked the idea of making up.

Production for season three of *Sex and the City* began shortly after the start of the year, and the early scripts indicated a giant step forward. Among the integral plotlines were an upcoming wedding for one of the women, a pregnancy for another, and a pair of suitors for Carrie. The fact that the creators of *Sex and the City* were taking big risks in a pivotal season was not lost on television and media observers. At this point, nobody would have blamed the show if, creatively, it treaded water for a little while.

The odyssey of these four women on the streets and in the bedrooms of New York City had been firmly established and structured. The new season could have easily evolved into a lot of intimate story lines that would have satisfied viewers. While the comedy element of the show remained intact, the emotional dimensions of the women deepened. Carrie's failed relationship with Mr. Big that concluded the second season was handled with seriousness but had hopeful tones. The wild, sexually free-spirited Samantha was beginning, albeit slightly, to address the consequences of her life as an older woman who was seemingly phobic about commitments. Miranda's cynicism and pickiness were coming into question. And finally Charlotte's longing for a white knight and a happy ending was severely tested. Further spicing up the proceedings was the introduction of actors Kyle McLachlan (of *Twin Peaks* fame) and John Corbett (another TV vet) as men who loved and tried to understand the *Sex and the City* women. In addition, a midseason trip to Los Angeles to film a pair of episodes was scheduled. While in Los Angeles, Sarah and her three costars had a moment of terror. During a scene in which Carrie and her friends were in a 1965 Mustang at the top of a steep hill, the car suddenly fell out of gear and began speeding down the hill. Sarah, at the wheel, managed to get the car under control and bring it to a stop.

Commenting on the evolution of the series, Sarah said she knew they were on a higher intellectual track when the traditional roles of men and women were reversed. She laughingly related that, when it was announced that John Corbett was going to come on the show as Carrie's new beau, all her fellow cast members said that they'd take him if she didn't want him. "All the men are objectified," Sarah told *TV Guide*. "They play the traditional woman's part. We just have our way with them and when we're done, next! Literally, some days you'll be in bed with two different men and you're like, 'Thank you so much; you were great. Next!'"

But in explaining what the third season had in store, Sarah admitted to the *New York Daily News* that she was anxious about a story line that was not going to show Carrie in the most positive light. "I think the audience is going to be conflicted about him [Corbett] and Carrie and Big. There's going to be behavior that people find troubling because it's troubling for us actors to play. There's going to be questions about Carrie's moral compass."

Easily the highlight of the season was the episode in which Carrie meets a lesbian, played by rock diva and Grammy Award winner Alanis Morissette, and ends up in a full-mouth kiss. Sarah took one look at the script and collapsed laughing at the ludicrousness of the situation, but once she stopped she began wondering how she was going to do this. Sarah had never kissed a woman before and did not know how she would react to it or even if she could do it. Once the press got wind of the story line, there were the usual outlandish rumors and innuendos. Sarah was reportedly refusing to do the pivotal scene and asking for a double. Matthew was reportedly perturbed that his wife had to kiss another woman. None of it was true. But it succeeded in being the best publicity the show could have. Producer Star assured Sarah that the kiss would be handled tastefully, and she was encouraged when she met Morissette and found her to be an unpretentious person who was having a lot of fun with the idea. Sarah decided that fun was the way to go. But on the day of the big kiss, Sarah was still completely at a loss as to how to kiss another woman. "I don't know what I was expecting," she related to the *Entertainment News Network*. "She [Morissette] did everything. I don't really kiss her. She kisses me and it's this thing, this moment, that just washes over Carrie. She was my first, so I'm glad it was her."

Sarah was starting to spend more time behind the scenes making decisions than in front of the camera. If there was a question regarding dialogue or motivation in a script, Sarah was there, as she was at most of the writers' story conferences. And the highest praise one could give her growing production skills was that in those story confabs she was treated as an equal. Writers would agree and disagree, argue their points with passion, and often press Sarah about why she thought something worked or not. Sarah, in response, would state her case in a simple, logical fashion (a trait she no doubt picked up from Matthew), and the creative tussle would continue. Being in front of the camera, Sarah knew what would work for her and her cast mates. And she would make her points like, well, a producer.

When it came to the clothes and hairstyles worn by the actors,

Sarah also took those responsibilities very seriously. One episode required a fleeting look at Carrie's open closet, and Sarah insisted that the clothes hanging inside be Carrie-specific—stylish rather than some bland stand-ins. When actor John Corbett balked at wearing a specific pair of pants during one episode, Sarah was nice but persistent, and he wore the pants. And although it was an unwritten rule, Sarah's insistence that none of the actors do commercials or other work that would cheapen their *Sex and the City* image was being followed. Sarah herself was selective in the commercials she chose. For instance, she had to think hard before she agreed to do the Nutrisse hair-color ads in 2000.

Like everything else about the show, Sarah's skills as a producer were starting to get noticed, especially in the theater community. Some theater owners wanted Sarah to produce some plays, and the highest compliment that she could receive was that nobody wanted her to star in them.

Matthew and Sarah had built a routine centered on her often hectic *Sex and the City* schedule. Sarah was always worried that Matthew would feel bad when he did not get a hot meal or when the laundry was piling up. He made every attempt to be at their apartment when Sarah was working. But inevitably there were days when Matthew was asleep when Sarah got home and still asleep when she left for work the next morning. As he once told *People*, he would find evidence of her having come home. "When I wake up I can see the newspapers spread out everywhere and an empty coffee cup, so I know she was there." When he was not out of town on a film shoot, Matthew was in the habit of stopping by the set and having lunch with Sarah. On more than one occasion, he happened on the set and saw actor Chris Noth or John Corbett walking around the set in a bathrobe, a sure sign that Sarah was shooting a bedroom scene. Where many husbands might have been jealous, Matthew was a true professional and understood that those scenes were just part of the job. After all, he was an actor too.

Adding to the excitement of the new season was the announcement that Sarah had been recognized by the television academy and given an Emmy nomination for Best Actress in a Comedy Series. She was once again passed over on awards night, but the defeat hardly registered as she happily mugged for photographers at a post-Emmy party given by HBO. The success of *Sex and the City* brought a sense of professional security for Sarah. It meant that the show was a proven winner in the eyes of HBO and that it would continue for some time. With enough episodes in the can, there was also some talk of syndication, but Sarah could not see *Sex and the City* on network TV—they would have to cut the heart out of it to make it palatable to mainstream America, although there were already brisk sales for the recent video release of the first season's episodes.

Being associated with a hit TV series meant that Sarah would be catapulted onto the short list of bankable motion picture actresses. She could pretty well plan her year around the show and make time for other things. Sarah and Matthew were homebodies who preferred to spend their free time together with family and friends.

A constant source of amusement for everybody but Sarah was the fact that Carrie was occasionally foulmouthed. An episode in which Sarah had to say the word "pussy" was a particular hardship. During the recording session, Sarah went through multiple takes as she struggled with what to her was an offensive term.

The perpetual rumor that Sarah and Matthew were starting a family was becoming more persistent, and it was beginning to concern the executives at HBO. It would be tough for the show to have the same impact on the show if Carrie were suddenly running around the streets of New York pregnant. It might be interesting, but it would not be *Sex and the City*. But Sarah assured the network that, while she was definitely going to start having children at some point, it was not in her immediate plans. At the same time, there was an obvious sense of frustration and sadness in her words. "I'm always worried that my time clock is ticking away," she candidly explained in *TV Guide*. "But I'm not going to think about it, and whatever happens happens. I have been advised by my women friends that life is more important."

Sarah had long been preoccupied with motherhood and had always had a sense of protectiveness when it came to children. She had a horror of violence, so it was no surprise that she got involved in certain charities. Midway through 2000, Sarah made an important political statement when she joined a group of celebrities in cutting commercials for the organization Handgun Control in which she told, in graphic, tearful detail, the tragic true story of a child who was killed by a handgun. Sarah also began devoting her energies to UNICEF and other charities with the goal of helping children.

To say that *Sex and the City* had become a cultural icon was an understatement. An estimated 10.6 million viewers—a lot by cable standards—were making the show a Sunday-night tradition. Parties were being thrown just to watch the show. Conversations around the water cooler at work dissected episodes. The cutting-edge nature of the show was also becoming a magnet for actors, such as Alec Baldwin, who would regularly call the producers for a guest appearance on the show. At one point, there was even talk of Matthew making an appearance. "I've had a couple of little chances," he told *TV Guide Insider*. "But it's never been where I was free at the right time. It just never worked out. But it might happen."

Another rumor at the time was that Sarah, during an upcoming hiatus, might reunite with Matthew in a television production of *The Music Man*. Matthew was cautiously optimistic but ultimately predicted that it would not happen because Sarah did not think it would be a good role for her. But he did think the couple would soon get together again, most likely in a television remake of *How to Succeed in Business without Really Trying*.

Sarah's ongoing antinudity edict had now stretched into its 21st year and had taken on legendary status in Hollywood. It had become a given, one propagated by Sarah, that at age 35 she was probably 10 years past her prime to appear nude even if she were willing. But the story began circulating that the producers of *Sex and the City* had offered Sarah a massive amount of money, reportedly in the neighborhood of $850,000, to appear nude in an episode of the series. In an interview with *Entertainment Tonight Online*, Sarah confirmed that the offer was real. And that she had, indeed, turned it down. "I think it's a business decision," she said. "I don't think they thought they were bribing me. I think they were just offering me enticing numbers, and those numbers were great. It's just so crazy. But for me it's a no-brainer. It's not a morality thing." But Sarah would also make it plain in various interviews that, if the story was right, the director was right, and the script was right, with nonexploitive nudity in it, she would seriously consider it.

As Carrie, Sarah had found her groove. Her performance remained grounded and sensible and fit the persona of Carrie. The banter could not have been more natural, and her sense of timing amid the frantic proceedings stood out in a subtle, multidimensional performance. At this juncture, Sarah was at home in the role and had made it her own.

With the conclusion of the third season of *Sex and the City*, Sarah turned to another film project, *State and Main*, the hilarious tale of what happens when a film company takes over a small New England town. The film was a heavy-duty ensemble piece that featured the likes of Alec Baldwin, William H. Macy, and Charles Durning. Her part, Claire, an pampered bimbo who disrupts the production when she refuses to appear topless, was an ironic reflection of Sarah's own antinudity stance as well as a legitimate acting challenge. And Sarah was thrilled to discover that the film would be directed and was written by the legendary David Mamet.

Auditioning for the Pulitzer Prize-winning playwright and director made Sarah uncharacteristically nervous. Happily, she discovered that Mamet—much like fellow playwright-director Harold Pinter had in *The Innocents* so many years before—projected an easygoing, somewhat fatherly persona. And although she recalled giving what she considered a very good read, Mamet was also auditioning her from another perspective. "He was more interested with me in the physical character," she told *Entertainment Tonight*. "How I held my head, and how I used my hands, and maybe that's the way to take the focus off the words." However, being number one on Mamet's list for *State and Main* did not stop Sarah from being nervous. "With Mamet, I was very, very nervous," she told *Harpers Bazaar*. "He uses biblical analogies when he's talking to you, so you really have to listen. He was the most polite director I've ever worked with. He thanks you after every shot."

The appeal for Sarah in *State and Main* was the freedom that being a part of a large ensemble cast offered her. She also liked the idea of working with the celebrated writer-director. She was confident that she could work in Mamet's world, and, although the first week of filming went well, Sarah was her own worst critic, and she did not think much of her performance. Part of the problem for Sarah was figuring out Mamet. He was big on spontaneous changes to the dialogue moments before a scene was to be shot. Was he doubting her abilities? Was *she* doubting her abilities? She didn't have an answer to Mamet's brand of shorthand, and it was driving her crazy. "After the first week of shooting, I went back to New York for the weekend, and I spent the entire time waiting for my phone to ring and for him to fire me," she recalled in the *New York Post*. "The phone didn't ring once, which shows you how popular I am."

Sarah returned to the *State and Main* location, but she was once again concerned when it came time for the scene in which her character strips to the bare essentials in an attempt to seduce the film's befuddled writer. The scene had been in the script since the beginning, but its implications had not been clear to her. Obviously, this ran contrary to Sarah's self-imposed ban on doing nudity. But this was David Mamet. How could she not get naked for one of the greatest dramatists of all time? "But it's important for the story for my character to appear as if she's naked, has no inhibitions," she told the *New York Post*. "I told Mr. Mamet I was concerned, and he said 'Don't worry. We'll figure it out on the set.'" Sarah did some figuring of her own and came up with a way to preserve her modesty. The resourceful actress took a man's T-shirt, cut out a square, and taped it snugly to the front of her body. When the scene was shot, Sarah wore a pair of shorts, but from the back it definitely looked like she was in the buff.

Given the comfortable nature of the shoot and the excellent chemistry between the actors, Sarah was more than willing to return to the role of actor. "Here I was just an actor for hire," she explained in an interview for the *Toronto Sun*. "Here I just came in and said: 'I will do whatever you want. Just tell me what to do and help me find my way.' It was terrifically liberating, as terrifying as it was. I loved working for him."

Sarah's confusion regarding Mamet's way of doing things and her fear that she was not performing up to his standards came full circle at the conclusion of filming when the director came up to her and said he had heard that she thought he was going to fire her. He just laughed. Sarah was nervous all over again. She need not have been, for her performance in *State and Main* is one of her most assured and well sculpted. Knowing that Claire is a send-up of her, she uses that as a driving force in a richly layered turn that draws on the clichés of the pampered, not-too-bright actress and recycles them in a polished, always enticing manner. Under Mamet's direction, the sequences between Sarah and William H. Macy as the harried producer generated laughs in a subtle, rather than a predictably flamboyant, manner. This was not a picture designed to let any one actor shine, but within the context of an all-star ensemble hers was easily a standout performance. Film critics tended to lump the entire cast together in their praise, but Sarah would get the occasional individual nod. *Rolling Stone*, in praising the film, described Sarah as "sly sexy."

Sarah took fond memories away from *State and Main*. The purist in her thought that playing in an ensemble cast was, in many ways, far more challenging than being the lead. She had learned from the other, often more experienced, actors. She had also liked the idea of figuratively being able to disappear into a crowd. These were mature notions for an actress in her mid-30s; they may also have been the subconscious tactics that would ensure a long career. Once again, Sarah was thinking ahead to a time when the bottom line would be her talent.

Sex and the City's growing popularity among a hip, young audience resulted in Sarah taking on one of her physically most demanding challenges—hosting the 2000 *MTV Movie Awards*. The hosting chores were not that difficult, but she had to make 15 costume changes during the awards show. Sarah would laugh nervously during commercial breaks as she struggled into yet another dress. By the end of the show, she was physically exhausted and went to her hotel room and fell asleep before she could get to the after-show party.

Late in 2000, Sarah was approached by *Harpers Bazaar* magazine to do an interview and a photo shoot for an upcoming issue. Part of the idea for the photo shoot was to expound on her long-held no-nudity clause in her *Sex and the City* contract by having her pose for some tasteful, partially nude shots. Sarah thought long and hard about whether to do the session. On one hand, it would give her an additional hint of sexuality that had not been present to that point in her career. On the other hand, the conservative-traditional streak in her made her shudder at the idea of appearing, even in a tasteful manner, on the cover of a magazine without any clothes on. After all, what would her mother think? Finally, she agreed to do the session, trusting implicitly in the photographer and the editor's insistence that nothing would be in bad taste. "I just lay there and did what I was told," she related in the February 2001 *Harpers Bazaar* article that accompanied the photos. "It was the most nude I have ever felt in my life."

Among the results of the shoot was the cover shot of Sarah wrapped enticingly in the American flag. Another shot had Sarah exercising in a striped bikini. And easily the most erotic photo was of the actress posed in nothing but a paint-sprayed shirt (strategically unbuttoned) and high heels. Sarah thought that the photo session did not exploit her, but she would reserve final judgment until the magazine came out. She did not think that the revealing photos would hurt her sweet-innocent image and that the sly sexuality the photos displayed would register on Hollywood and allow her to explore more diversified roles. Sarah was somewhat nervous about the impending arrival of the magazine with her

revealing photo on the cover. But the pictures were a high-gloss, tasteful reflection of her beauty. In the days that followed, the response was overwhelmingly positive.

In the meantime, Sarah was finding much to occupy her professionally. She took a central role in the dark comedy *Life without Dick* and agreed to coproduce the film version of the Off Broadway play *Fuddy Meers*. The latter project was a particular delight and challenge. Her experience in the theater, both good and bad, had given her insights into the psyches of actors and directors, which made her casting choices well thought out. Admittedly, the logistics, monetary and physical, of putting on a play were new to her, but she had learned much about the dollars and cents from producing *Sex and the City*, which helped her to finally make enlightened choices and decisions.

Her growing stardom also began to bring in other, nontraditional types of offers. Sarah willingly jumped at the chance to do a cameo in the small but star-studded comedy based on the life of Jacqueline Susann, *Isn't She Great*. She was also honored to be asked to be interviewed as part of a moving TV documentary tribute to one of her favorite actors, Madeline Kahn, in *Intimate Portrait*. But easily one of the most bizarre offers, and one she accepted, was from Priceline.com, the gateway to comparative shopping. William Shatner jump-started his career through a series of hilarious live commercials, but when he left, Priceline.com decided to go in a different direction in 2001. For the animated commercial in which an upscale woman leads a fantasy life, it needed a spunky yet sophisticated voice. Recalling her days as voice-over queen in her childhood, Sarah was interested and did the voice-over work for the series of commercials that began airing in the new year.

But more than ever, with the flood of interesting offers coming her way, Sarah was grateful for the private time. The *Sex and the City* notoriety was now making it difficult for Matthew and her to go out in public without being approached. But the couple were insistent on not allowing their lives to be disrupted by their success, so they continued to take the attention in stride. And the question of when Sarah and Matthew would have children once again began to pop up in the media. Finally, in an interview with the European magazine *Solo*, Sarah acknowledged that they were actually in the process of answering the question. She would also acknowledge in a subsequent talk with *ICShowbiz.com* that ideally she would like to have three children. "We are really trying," she announced. "But it's not easy. We both work a lot, and when there are only two good days of the month to get pregnant in, that takes some luck too. My friends who have children always say that kids are a lot more important than all the careers in the world, and that you don't have your whole life to start a family. I trust them, so we're doing our best and hoping for luck."

During an interview with the *New York Daily News* about his appearance for *Night Must Fall*, Matthew thought he was actually going to get through an entire conversation without having to deal with the baby question. But when it finally came, the actor jokingly stated his case for possible parenthood. "I'm not sure what I'm supposed to say," he laughed. "I can't remember our rule at the moment. I would like to have children. Might as well if you're going to be alive. I mean it's part of life. I'm scared of them a little. They require a lot of attention, I'm told. But they're cute."

Age was also becoming a factor in Sarah's professional life as she and her fellow cast mates began preparing for the fourth season of *Sex and the City*. Although the show was not displaying any signs of flagging in popularity, these characters were aging, and some of the elements of the series might become unbelievable as the characters got into their forties and beyond. "These women are getting older and older," Sarah agreed in a *Solo* conversation. "And in some way, we have to choose how to handle that. I don't want the show to evolve into something that will have to be renamed *Please Have Sex With Me in the City* or *Seniors in the City*." But despite her anxious musings, at age 35 Sarah had to admit that she had a few good years left, as did the show.

Her confidence in *Sex and the City* was once again rewarded when the prestigious Golden Globe Awards, presented by the Hollywood Foreign Press Association, announced their nominees.

Sex and the City was named on the short list of Best Television Series, and Sarah lit up at the announcement that she had been nominated for Best Performance by an Actress in a Television Series—Comedy/Musical.

The days and weeks leading up to the awards ceremony were a busy and exciting time for Sarah. On the one hand, she was attempting to lead a normal life with Matthew. Her idea of unwinding was to cook for large gatherings of family and friends, and when not in the kitchen she was reading the early scripts for season four of *Sex and the City*. Sarah was happy with the way the show was consistently growing in interesting and humorous ways, and she did not agree with those who thought that *Sex and the City* would have to get more and more graphic until it pushed the boundaries of taste too far. She has often explained that the writers know exactly what the boundaries are and that there are still new revelations and new areas to explore within those limits. She has assured critics that the show will never become predictable and redundant.

Even though the new season of *Sex and the City* was next on her agenda, Sarah would regularly entertain new movie proposals and would often be found in her living room reading through scripts. And as a suddenly bankable star on the rise, she was often finding the frustration that other reigning cinema queens must have felt. "I love the adventure of making movies, going someplace new, and discovering new things," she told the *National Post*. "But I read film scripts every day, and I never see anything as complicated, truthful, and interesting as the characters on our show."

Matthew and Sarah ended 2000 on a high note. They were happily in love and were professionally and personally fulfilled. January was Golden Globes month, and Sarah had been nominated again. Could she possibly carry off back-to-back wins? Sarah was doubtful. She was up against Calista Flockhart, whose hit series *Ally McBeal* had been revived by Sarah's former lover Robert Downey Jr.'s guest appearances. Then there was Jane Kaczmarck in *Malcolm in the Middle* and the gorgeous Debra Messing of

Will & Grace. Finally there was Hollywood legend Bette Midler.

It was an anxious pre-awards dinner. Sarah, who usually ate heartily, just picked at her food. Luckily, her category would be announced early in the show. The time came, and to her utter disbelief, her name was announced. She had done it—two in a row! She tried to compose herself. As she made her way to the stage, Sarah was a knockout in her pink Oscar de la Renta dress and her "lucky" earrings. They were the huge silver sparklers that she had worn the previous year for her first Golden Globe. Her acceptance speech was a little better than her awkward stammering the year before, but it was far from a polished effort. "I'm ill-prepared again. It's like high school." Needless to say, she'd passed the test.

Sarah continued to field a variety of offers, and one of the most enticing was to star in the theater production of *Wonders of the World*, a dark comedy in which an unhappy woman flees her marriage only to meet up with a suicidal alcoholic who is debating whether to ride over a waterfall in a huge jar of peanut butter. Sarah was interested in playing the lead but saw a conflict with the upcoming season of *Sex and the City*. The producers agreed to push the play back in order to accommodate Sarah, and negotiations went on for a projected July 2001 premiere at the famed Manhattan Theater Club.

The odyssey through her professional and personal lives had seen many dips, stumbles, and falls, but Sarah had learned from all of those experiences. Well into 2001, she was at the top of her profession and content in her relationship. Sarah had evolved into a pop culture icon. Her striking, unique beauty and hip, albeit tentative, sensibilities had turned her into a heroine for all seasons. That she had managed to remain largely unfazed by the accolades and attention and continued to present a natural, unaffected face to the world were a big part of the attraction. So was the fact that she had managed a persona that was at once smoldering sexuality and real world in a way that was small town, like Nelsonville, Ohio.

The future for Sarah Jessica Parker is a happy mystery. Children are definitely on her agenda, and the consensus is that she will be

Sarah wins back-to-back Golden Globe Awards

a mother within the next few years. Her prowess as an actress who can literally do it all will assure her of an ever-widening array of acting challenges. And there is already an indication that she will become a power behind the scenes as producer and perhaps director and writer. And she has remained human, likable, and totally unaffected by her fairy-tale life in Hollywood. Sarah's Cinderella story has one big happy ending. But was the best yet to come? Suddenly, the phone rang, and Sarah picked it up. The voice at the other end asked her if she would like to be a presenter at the 73rd annual Academy Awards. The Academy Awards! Of course, Sarah jumped at the chance. What an honor. Perhaps the best really was yet to come.

 Performance Credits

Major Theater Credits

THE INNOCENTS
(1976)
Sarah played the role of Flora.

ANNIE
(1979-81)
Sarah played an orphan during her first year and Annie for the final two years.

TO GILLIAN ON HER 37TH BIRTHDAY
(1983-84)
Sarah played the role of Rachel.

THE HEIDI CHRONICLES
(1989)
Sarah played the roles of Becky, Clara, and Denise.

THE SUBSTANCE OF FIRE
(1991-92)
Sarah played the role of Sarah Geldhart.

SYLVIA
(1995)
Sarah played the role of Sylvia.

HOW TO SUCCEED IN BUSINESS WITHOUT REALLY TRYING
(1996)
Sarah played the role of Rosemary Pilkington.

ONCE UPON A MATTRESS
(1996-97)
Sarah played the role of Princess Winnifred.

Television Series

SQUARE PEGS
(1982-83)
Producer: Luciano Martino
Director: Various
Writer: Various
Sarah plays the role of Patty Greene.

A YEAR IN THE LIFE
(1987-88)
Producer: Stephen Cragg
Director: Stephen Cragg
Writer: Various
Sarah plays the role of Kay Ericson Gardner.

EQUAL JUSTICE
(1990)
Producer: Thomas Carter
Director: Various
Writer: Various
Sarah plays the role of Jo Ann Harris.

SEX AND THE CITY
(1998-)
Producer: Darren Star, Michael Patrick King, Barry Jossen, Sarah Jessica
           Parker
Director: Various
Writer: Various
Sarah plays the role of Carrie Bradshaw.

Television Movies and Miniseries

MY BODY, MY CHILD
(1982)
Producer: Robert Berger, Herbert Brodkin, Thomas De Wolfe
Director: Marvin J. Chomsky
Writer: Louise Burns-Bisogno
Sarah plays the role of Katy.

GOING FOR THE GOLD: THE BILL JOHNSON STORY
(1985)
Producer: Gary Goodman, Barry Rosen
Director: Don Taylor
Sarah plays the role of Bill Johnson's girlfriend.

A YEAR IN THE LIFE
(1986)
Producer: Stephen Cragg
Director: Thomas Carter
Writer: Josh Brand, John Falsey, Stu Krieger
Sarah plays the role of Kay Ericson.

THE ROOM UPSTAIRS
(1987)
Producer: Robert Huddleston, Marian Rees
Director: Stuart Margolin
Writer: Steve Lawson, Norma Levinson
Sarah plays the role of Mandy.

DADAH IS DEATH
(1988)
Producer: Matt Carroll, Steve Krantz
Director: Jerry London
Writer: Bill Kerby
Sarah plays the role of Rachel.

TWIST OF FATE
(1989)
Producer: Larry White
Director: Ian Sharp
Writer: William Bast, Paul Huson, Jules Schwerin, Robert L. Fish
Sarah plays the role of Miriam.

THE RYAN WHITE STORY
(1989)
Producer: Alan Landsberg, Linda Otto
Director: John Herzfeld
Writer: Phil Pennigroth, John Herzfeld
Sarah plays an unnamed role.

IN THE BEST INTEREST OF THE CHILDREN
(1992)
Producer: Paul Freeman, Michael Ray Rhodes
Director: Michael Ray Rhodes
Writer: Peter Nelson, Jud Kinberg
Sarah plays the role of Callie Cain.

THE SUNSHINE BOYS
(1995)
Producer: John Erman, Robert Halmi, Gerrit Van Der Meer
Director: John Erman
Writer: Neil Simon
Sarah plays the role of Nancy Clark.

Filmography (Theatrical)

RICH KIDS
(1979)
Producer: Robert Altman, George W. George, Michael Hausman
Director: Robert M. Young
Writer: Judith Ross
Sarah plays an unnamed teenager.

SOMEWHERE TOMORROW
(1983)

Producer: Glenn Kershaw, Robert Wiemer
Director: Robert Wiemer
Writer: Robert Wiemer

Sarah plays the role of Lori Anderson.

FOOTLOOSE
(1984)

Producer: Daniel Melnick, Lewis J. Rachmil, Craig Zadan
Director: Herbert Ross
Writer: Dean Pitchford

Sarah plays the role of Rusty.

FIRSTBORN
(1984)

Producer: Stanley R. Jaffe, Paul Junger Witt, Ron Koslow, Sherry
Lansing, Tony Thomas, Alice Shure
Director: Michael Apted
Writer: Ron Koslow

Sarah plays the role of Lisa.

GIRLS JUST WANT TO HAVE FUN
(1985)

Producer: Stuart Cornfeld, James G. Robinson, Chuck Russell
Director: Alan Metter
Writer: Janis Hirsch, Amy Spies

Sarah plays the role of Janey Glenn.

FLIGHT OF THE NAVIGATOR
(1986)

Producer: Mark Damon, Malcolm L. Harden, John W. Hyde, David
Joseph, Jonathan Sanger, Dimitri Villard, Robby Wold
Director: Randal Kleiser
Writer: Mark H. Baker, Michael Burton, Matt MacManus

Sarah plays the role of Carolyn McAdams.

L.A. STORY
(1991)
Producer: Mario Kassar, Steve Martin, Daniel Melnick, Michael I.
   Rachmil
Director: Mick Jackson
Writer: Steve Martin
Sarah plays the role of SanDeE.

HONEYMOON IN VEGAS
(1992)
Producer: Mike Lobell, Neil A. Machlis, Adam Merims
Director: Andrew Bergman
Writer: Andrew Bergman
Sarah plays the role of Betsy/Donna.

HOCUS POCUS
(1993)
Producer: Mick Garris, Bonnie Bruckheimer, Ralph Winter, Steven
   Haft, Jay Heit, David Kirschner
Director: Kenny Ortega
Writer: Mick Garris, Neil Cuthbert, David Kirschner, Kenny Ortega,
   Greg Beeman
Sarah plays the role of Sarah Sanderson.

STRIKING DISTANCE
(1993)
Producer: Steve Reuther, Carmine Zozzora, Hunt Lowry, Arnon
   Milchan, Marty Kaplan, Tony Thomopoulos.
Director: Rowdy Herrington
Writer: Rowdy Herrington, Marty Kaplan
Sarah plays the role of Emily Harper.

ED WOOD
(1994)
Producer: Tim Burton, Denise Di Novi, Michael Lehmann, Michael
   Flynn
Director: Tim Burton
Writer: Scott Alexander, Larry Karaszewski, Rudolph Grey
Sarah plays the role of Delores Fuller.

MIAMI RHAPSODY
(1995)

Producer: Jon Avnet, Jordan Kerner, David Frankel, Barry Jossen, Joe M. Aguilar, Noah Ackerman
Director: David Frankel
Writer: David Frankel
Sarah plays the role of Gwyn Marcus.

THE FIRST WIVES CLUB
(1996)

Producer: Adam Schroeder, Ezra Swerdlow, Noah Ackerman, Thomas Imperato, Heather Nicky, Craig Perry, Scott Rudin
Director: Hugh Wilson
Writer: Olivia Goldsmith, Robert Harling
Sarah plays the role of Shelly Stewart.

IF LUCY FELL
(1996)

Producer: Eric Schaeffer, Deborah Ridpath, Terence Michael, Adam Brightman, Bradley Jenkel, Brad Krevoy, Steven Stabler
Director: Eric Schaeffer
Writer: Eric Schaeffer, Tony Spiridakis
Sarah plays the role of Lucy Ackerman.

THE SUBSTANCE OF FIRE
(1996)

Producer: Jon Robin Baitz, Lemore Syvan, Randy Finch, Ron Kastner
Director: Daniel J. Sullivan
Writer: Jon Robin Baitz
Sarah plays the role of Sarah Geldhart.

EXTREME MEASURES
(1996)

Producer: Elizabeth Hurley, Andrew Scheinman, Chris Brigham, Jeanney Kim
Director: Michael Apted
Writer: Michael Palmer, Tony Gilroy
Sarah plays the role of Jodie Trammel.

MARS ATTACKS!
(1996)
Producer: Tim Burton, Larry J. Franco, Paul Deason, Mark S. Miller
Director: Tim Burton
Writer: Jonathan Gems
Sarah plays the role of Nathalie Lake.

'TIL THERE WAS YOU
(1997)
Producer: Sigurjon Sighvatsson, Ted Tannebaum, Penny Finkelman-
    Cox, Alan Paul, Julie Golden, James McQuaide, Tom
    Rosenberg, Richard S. Wright
Director: Scott Winant
Writer: Winnie Holzman
Sarah plays the role of Francesca Lanfield.

A LIFE APART: HASIDISM IN AMERICA
(1997)
Producer: Menachem Daum, Arnold Labaton
Director: Menachem Daum, Oren Rudavsky
Writer: Menachem Daum, Robert Seidman
Sarah is co-narrator with Leonard Nimoy.

DUDLEY DO-RIGHT
(1999)
Producer: Hugh Wilson, Warren Carr, John Davis, J. Todd Harris,
    A. Ideth Hernandez, Mary Kane, Carmen More, Joseph
    Singer, Kathy Zimmer
Director: Hugh Wilson
Writer: Hugh Wilson, Jay Ward
Sarah plays the role of Nell Fenwick.

ISN'T SHE GREAT
(2000)
Producer: Mark Gordon, Ted Kurdyla, Gary Levinsohn, Mike Lobell,
    Cathy Schulman
Director: Andrew Bergman
Writer: Paul Rudnick, Michael Korda
Sarah plays the role of Tira Gropman.

STATE AND MAIN
(2000)

Producer: Alec Baldwin, Martin J. Barab, Jonathan Cornick, Peter Jay
        Klauser, Sarah Green, Rachel Horovitz, Alan Mruvka, Mark
        Ordesky, Dorothy Aufiero
Director: David Mamet
Writer: David Mamet

Sarah plays the role of Claire Wellesley.

INTIMATE PORTRAIT: MADELINE KAHN
(2000)

Producer: Donna Edge-Rachell, Joseph Feury
Director: Lee Grant
Writer: Donna Edge-Rachell

Sarah was interviewed for the documentary.

LIFE WITHOUT DICK
Producer: Illeana Douglas
Director: Bix Skahill
Writer: Bix Skahill

Sarah plays the role of Pauline.

Bibliography

Special thanks to Mark Fossitt for his valuable research into European coverage of Sarah Jessica Parker.

Books

Current Biography Yearbook. New York: H.W. Wilson, 1998.

Harris Roy. *Eight Women of the American Stage: Talking about Acting*. Portsmouth, NH: Heinemann, 1997.

Leonard Maltin's Movie and Video Guide. New York: Penguin, 1997.

McNeil, Alex. *Total Television: A Comprehensive Guide to Programming from 1948 to the Present*. New York: Penguin, 1991.

Trotter, David. *Videohound's Golden Movie Retriever*. Detroit: Visible Ink Press, 1993.

Web Sites

E! Online www.eonline.com.

Entertainment Tonight Online www.etonline.com.

IC Showbiz icshowbiz.ic24.com.

The Independent Online www.peconic.ne:0080.independent/07039610. htm.

Internet Movie Database (IMDb) http://us.imdb.com.

Mr. Showbiz www.mrshowbiz.go.com/sarahjessicaparker/content/news. htm.

National Post Online www.nationalpost.com.
New York Post www.nypost.com.
Playbill On-Line www.playbill.com.
The Sarah Jessica Parker Theater Page www.geocities.com/hollywood/
    5159/theater.htm.
TNT Rough Cuts http://tnt.turner.com.
TV Guide Online www.tvguide.com.
World Entertainment News Network www.wenn.com.
Zap2It.com www.zap2it.com.

Magazines, Newspapers, and On-Line Stories

Alford, Henry. "Head over Heels." *Harper's Bazaar* Feb. 2001.
Aurora. "What Happened to Me in the Last Few Years Is Incredible."
    Aftonbladet TV 21 Nov. 2000.
——. "Solo Cover Story." *Solo* Nov. 2000.
Ausiello, Michael. "Will Matthew and Sarah Make Music Together?"
    TV Guide Online 8 Nov. 2000.
Bianculli, David. "To Sex Star Dave Is Her Mr. Big." *New York Daily
    News* 25 May 2000.
——. "The Dirtiest Girls on TV." *New York Daily News* 28 May 2000.
Bonin, Liane. "Couples Therapy." *Entertainment Weekly* 30 Aug. 1999.
Buskirk, Leslie Van. "The Best Year of Her Life." *US* 2 Nov. 1984.
Cagle, Jess. "Sarah Jessica Parker . . . What Kind of a Household Name
    Is That?" *Entertainment Weekly* 10 Jan. 1993.
Caulfield, Deborah. "Girls Just Want to Have Fun off Screen Too." *Los
    Angeles Times* 16 May 1985.
Cole, Stephen. "Don't Even Try to Beat David Mamet at Verbal Ping
    Pong." *National Post* 9 Sept. 2000.
Connolly, Sheryl. "Matt Goes into Action." *New York Daily News* 24 May
    1998.
Daspin, Eileen. "The Divine Sarah." *W Magazine* Sept. 1994.
De Jounge, Peter. "The Real Sarah Jessica Parker." *Harpers Bazaar* Oct.
    1994.
Dickson, Kevin. "Sex Appeal: Sarah Jessica Parker on Sex, the City, and
    a Whole Lot More." *TV Guide Canada* www.entertainmentnews
    daily.com.

Diliberto, Gioia. "Scarcely out of Their Teens, Sarah Jessica Parker and Robert Downey Play House in Hollywood." *People* 30 Sept. 1985.

Dunn, Janice. "Talk of the Town." *US* Feb. 1995.

Evans, Hilary. "Star of Stage, TV, and Screen and Just Barely out of Her Teens." *Los Angeles Herald Examiner* 21 Apr. 1985.

Fabrikant, Geraldine. "From a Start on Welfare to Riches in the City." *New York Times* 30 July 2000.

Frankel, Martha. "How Sarah Jessica Parker Found Happiness Ever After." *Redbook* Sept. 1997.

Frascella, Larry. "Sarah Jessica Parker Goes Steady." *Model* May 1997.

Henderson, Kathy. "In Her Best Interest." *Los Angeles Times* 16 Feb. 1992.

Hofler, Robert. "City Dweller Parker Eyes New World." *Variety* 1 Feb. 2000.

Honeycutt, Kirk. "The Delightful Upswing of Robert Downey Jr." *Cosmopolitan* Sept. 1990.

Hruska, Bronwen. "The Sunshine Girl." *Los Angeles Times* 3 Mar. 1996.

"I've Been Offered a Lot More than That to Do Nudity." *Entertainment Tonight.* Dec. 2000.

Jacobs, A.J. "Let's Talk about Sex." *Entertainment Weekly* 5 June 1998.

Jicha, Tom. "Sex and the City Star Considers Herself Less Racy than Her Character." *Philadelphia Inquirer* 22 Jan. 1999.

Jones, Andy. "Sexy Sarah." TNT Rough Cuts 1999 http://tnt.turner.com.

Kelly, Christina. "Just One of the Girls." *New Woman* Dec. 1996.

Kennedy, Dana. "Sex Appeal." *TV Guide Online* 2 Feb. 2001.

Kirkland, Bruce. "Parker Gives In." *Toronto Sun* 9 Sept. 2000.

Lee, Luaine. "Sarah Jessica Parker Forsakes Sewing for Sex." *St. Louis Post-Dispatch* 23 Aug. 1998.

LeRoy, Bridget. "Sarah Jessica Parker." *Independent Online* 1996.

Lipton, Michael A. "City Limits." *People* 8 Nov. 1999.

Lumenick, Lou. "Double Parker." *New York Post* 17 Dec. 2000.

Marshall, Sharon. "Sarah Longs to Be a Mum." *IC Showbiz.com* 21 Feb. 1999.

Nathan, Jean. "A Shaggy Dog Story with a Cast That's Altogether Human." *New York Times* 21 May 1995.

"New Sex Season for Parker." *Zap2It.com.* 30 May 2000.

O'Neill, Anne Marie. "Naughty but Nice." *People* 2 Oct. 2000.

Rea, Steven. "A Veteran of Filmdom and Still Unexposed." *Philadelphia Inquirer* 31 Dec. 2000.

Riedel, Michael. "Anger Springs up over Mattress." *New York Daily News* 11 Dec. 1996.

——. "Is Sarah Tony Shy?" *New York Daily News* 11 Dec. 1996.

Roher, Trish Deitch. "Downey Time." *Mirabella* Feb. 1991.

Sikes, Gini. "Sex and the Cynical Girl: A Cynical Approach." *New York Times* 5 Apr. 1998.

Spavin, Vicky. "Sarah Safe in the City." *IC Showbiz.com* 13 Sept. 2000.

Specter, Michael. "Bimbo? Sarah Jessica Parker Begs to Differ." *New York Times* 20 Sept. 1992.

Strauss, Bob. "Sarah Jessica Parker Hits High Notes in Her Personal, Professional Lives." *Los Angeles Daily News* 1 Sept. 1999.

St. Nicholas, Randee. "Sarah Smile." *US* 21 Feb. 1991.

Szebin, Fred. "Back with Tim Burton." *Femme Fatales* Feb. 1997.

Tannenbaum, Rob. "Bewitched." *GQ* July 1993.

Vellela, Tony. "Sarah Jessica Parker Revisits Musical Roots." *Christian Science Monitor* 21 Jan. 1997.

Young, Paul. "Rebel with a Cause." *Buzz* 1997 Jul.-Aug. 1992.

Weber, Bruce. "Too Cute for Words?" *New York Times* 25 Apr. 1996.

Weintraub, Bernard. "On Stardom, Dating, and the Baby She'd Love to Have." *Redbook* July 1996.

White, Garrett. "Hollywood Hopes Her Career's Going Great but Sarah Jessica Parker Can't Wait To Get Married." 21 Aug. 1992.

Winer, Laurie. "Sarah Jessica Parker." *Redbook* Oct. 1999.